Weapons Of Our Warfare

Overcoming By Gods Promises

Dr Michael h Yeager

All rights reserved. No part of this book is allowed to be reproduced, stored in a retrieval system, or transmitted by any form or by any means-electronic, mechanical, photocopy, recording, or otherwise-without prior written permission of the copyright owner, except by a reviewer who wishes to quote brief passages in connection with a review for inclusion in a magazine, website, newspaper, podcast, or broadcast. All Scripture quotations, unless otherwise indicated, are taken from the King James Authorized Version of the Bible.

(Some of the teaching in this book is partly taken from the Adam Clarke Commentary, and other non-copy right or copy right acknowledged material found on the internet)

Copyright © 2016 Dr Michael H Yeager

All rights reserved.

ISBN:1530069254
ISBN-13:9781530069255

DEDICATION

All of the Scriptures used in this meditation book is from the original 1611 version of the King James Bible. I give thanks to God the Father , Jesus Christ and the Holy Ghost for the powerful impact the word has had upon my life. Without the word Quicken in my heart by the Holy Ghost I would've been lost and I'm done. To the Lord of Heaven and Earth I am eternally indebted for his great love and his mercy, his protections and his provisions, his divine guidance and overwhelming goodness. To him be glory and praise for ever and ever: Amen .

CONTENTS

  Acknowledgments i

1 **Chapter One** **1**
  This Is WAR!
  Ignorance Will Kill You
  Understanding God
  Jesus Christ
  Understanding Your Enemy
  We Are Soldiers

2 **Chapter Two** **15**
  The Believers Armor
  Overcoming By God's Promises
  Weapons Of War
  We Must Meditate
  What Is Meditation?
  The Holy Ghost

3 **Chapter Three** **31**
  Looking At Our Armor
  Loins Girt about with Truth
  Breastplate Of Righteousness
  Shoes of the Gospel of Peace
  The Shield Of Faith

4 **Chapter Four** **47**
  The Helmet of Salvation
  The sword of the Spirit
  Praying Always with All Prayer
  Gods Mighty Men

5 **Chapter Five** **63**
  The Name of the LORD
  It Is Written
  The Divine Nature
  18 Important Characteristics
  Diligence
  Faithfulness
  Virtue
  Knowledge

6 **Chapter Six** **81**
  Temperance
  Patience
  Godliness
  Brotherly kindness
  Charity
  Joy

7	**Chapter Seven**	97
	Goodness	
	Meekness	
	Peace Makers	
	Longsuffering	
	Gentleness	
	Holiness	
	Mercy	
	Reverence	
8	**Chapter Eight**	113
	Offensive Weapons	
	Having a Vision	
	Knowing Your Purpose	
	Walking In The Spirit	
	Authority & Power	
	Complete Agreement	
	Divine Guidance	
	We Must Overcome	
9	**Chapter Nine**	129
	Defensive Weapons	
	Divine Healing	
	Divine Protection	
	Praise, Worship, Thanksgiving,	
	Divine Provisions	
	God's Grace	
10	**Chapter Ten**	143
	Adversity	
	Anger	
	Comfort	
	Dependability	
	Duty	
	Encouragement	
	Generosity	
	Gratitude	
	Justice	
	Labor	
	Repentance	
	Righteousness	
	Salvation	
	Seeking God	
	Selfishness	
	Sin	
	Temptations	
	Unity	
	Wisdom	

ACKNOWLEDGMENTS

*To our heavenly Father and His wonderful love.

*To our Lord, Savior and Master —Jesus Christ, Who saved us and set us free because of His great love for us.

*To the Holy Spirit, Who leads and guides us into the realm of miraculous living every day.

*To all of those who had a part in helping us get this book ready for the publishers.

*To our precious children, Michael, Daniel, Steven, Stephanie, Catherine Yu, who is our precious daughter-in-law, and Naomi, who is now with the Lord.

CHAPTER ONE

Importance of This Book

This book is written to equip you to do battle. Every Scripture I share in this book is with the intent of it being **Memorized** and **Meditated** upon. In order for you to enjoy the victory that **Christ Jesus** has already obtained for you, it is necessary for you to hide the Scriptures in your **heart**, these truths, these realities, in order to overcome The World, The Flesh, and The Devil! There are over **7000 promises** given to the believer in the word of God. The Scriptures I share in this book are a very small portion of those wonderful, exceedingly great, and precious promises. I cannot cover in this one book all of the weapons that God has given to us, but I will give to you the basic truths of God's word that will equip you to overcome the enemy of your soul. **I Strongly Suggests You Pick Three Out of Each Section to Memorize, And Meditate On! Pick the three, and high light them in yellow!**

*Please take these Scriptures seriously!

This Is WAR!

*****Revelation 12:7 And there was war in heaven: Michael and his angels fought against the dragon; and the dragon fought and his angels,**

There is a war that is raging all around us. It began in the book of Genesis, and we see its completion in the very last chapter of the book of Revelation. The word **war** is used 220 times in the Bible, **battle** 171 times, **fight** 103 times, **Army** 73 times. This is a supernatural warfare, a conflict, a battle with to opposing sides. As a human being you are either in the fight with God against the powers of darkness, or you have been made a captive, a prisoner, a victim of demonic forces.

*****2 Timothy 2:25 In meekness instructing those that oppose themselves; if God peradventure will give them repentance to the acknowledging of the**

truth;26 And that they may recover themselves out of the snare of the devil, who are taken captive by him at his will.

---

*Ephesians 6:12 - For we wrestle not against flesh and blood, but against principalities, against powers, against the rulers of the darkness of this world, against spiritual wickedness in high [places].

---

*I2 Corinthians 10:3-5 - For though we walk in the flesh, we do not war after the flesh:

---

*Ephesians 6:13 - Wherefore take unto you the whole armour of God, that ye may be able to withstand in the evil day, and having done all, to stand.

---

*Deuteronomy 28:7 - The LORD shall cause thine enemies that rise up against thee to be smitten before thy face: they shall come out against thee one way, and flee before thee seven ways.

---

*2 Corinthians 10:4 (For the weapons of our warfare are not carnal, but mighty through God to the pulling down of strong holds;)

---

*1 Timothy 1:18 This charge I commit unto thee, son Timothy, according to the prophecies which went before on thee, that thou by them mightest war a good warfare;

---

*Proverbs 24:6 For by wise counsel thou shalt make thy war: and in multitude of counsellors there is safety.

---

*2 Timothy 2:4 No man that warreth entangleth himself with the affairs of this life; that he may please him who hath chosen him to be a soldier.

---

*1 Peter 2:11 Dearly beloved, I beseech you as strangers and pilgrims, abstain from fleshly lusts, which war against the soul;

---

*Revelation 17:14 These shall make war with the Lamb, and the Lamb shall overcome them: for he is Lord of lords, and King of kings: and they that are with him are called, and chosen, and faithful.

Ignorance Will Kill You!

Being sincere will not help you in the midst of the battle. Untold numbers have been destroyed because they had no knowledge. You might say that they were shooting into the dark. Completely oblivious and blind to the fact of what was going on in the spiritual realm. That's why Jesus proclaimed boldly: **you shall know the truth, and the truth will make you free.** Many who proclaim to know Christ are completely ignorant and blind to how God works. A good example of this is when Eve was being tempted of the devil. Why did God not come to her help? Here is the simple answer: she did not cry out, and ask for his help! If she would have simply cried out to God, and asked for his help, he would have been there faster than you could snap your fingers. Many have accused God of horrendous crimes because they did not know their adversary, and did not understand who God really is, or how he works.

*Hosea 4:6 My people are destroyed for lack of knowledge: because thou hast rejected knowledge, I will also reject thee, that thou shalt be no priest to me: seeing thou hast forgotten the law of thy God, I will also forget thy children.

*Isaiah 5:13 Therefore my people are gone into captivity, because they have no knowledge: and their honourable men are famished, and their multitude dried up with thirst.

*Isaiah 1:3 The ox knoweth his owner, and the ass his master's crib: but Israel doth not know, my people doth not consider.

*2 Corinthians 4:3 But if our gospel be hid, it is hid to them that are lost:4 In whom the god of this world hath blinded the minds of them which believe not, (the word of God) **lest the light of the glorious gospel of Christ, who is the image of God, should shine unto them.5 For we preach not ourselves, but Christ Jesus the Lord; and ourselves your servants for Jesus' sake.**

*Hosea 4:4 Hear the word of the Lord, ye children of Israel: for the Lord hath a controversy with the inhabitants of the land, because there is no truth, nor mercy, nor knowledge of God in the land.

*2 Peter 3:5 For this they willingly are ignorant of, that by the word of God the heavens were of old, and the earth standing out of the water and in the water:

*James 1:13 Let no man say when he is tempted, I am tempted of God: for God cannot be tempted with evil, neither tempteth he any man:

*James 4:2 Ye lust, and have not: ye kill, and desire to have, and cannot obtain: ye fight and war, yet ye have not, because ye ask not.***Job 42:2** I know that thou canst do everything, and that no thought can be withholden from thee.3 Who is he that hideth counsel without knowledge? therefore have I uttered that I understood not; things too wonderful for me, which I knew not...........5 I have heard of thee by the hearing of the ear: but now mine eye seeth thee.6 Wherefore I abhor myself, and repent in dust and ashes.

*2 Corinthians 11:3 But I fear, lest by any means, as the serpent beguiled Eve through his subtilty, so your minds should be corrupted from the simplicity that is in Christ.

*2 Corinthians 2:11 Lest Satan should get an advantage of us: for we are not ignorant of his devices.

Understanding God!

God has given us his word for one reason, and that is to know him. To know God, is to love God. There are so many Scriptures that boldly declare unto **US who God is** in his goodness, mercy, love, forgiveness, divine attributes, and nature. In this book I am simply giving you a small portion but powerful hand set of Scriptures in order to help you overcome the lies of the devil. These Scriptures which God has provided will cause you to be able to live a victorious, wonderful, overcoming and beautiful life. Please take the time to hide these Scriptures in your heart. They will convert your soul, renew your mind, transform you, and translate you into an amazing heavenly realm.

*Malachi 3:6 For I am the Lord, I change not; therefore ye sons of Jacob are not consumed.

* Numbers 23:19 God is not a man, that he should lie; neither the son of man, that he should repent: hath he said, and shall he not do it? or hath he spoken, and shall he not make it good?

*James 1:17 Every good gift and every perfect gift is from above, and cometh down from the Father of lights, with whom is no variableness, neither shadow of turning.*Lamentations 3:22 It is of the Lord's mercies that we are not consumed, because his compassions fail not.

*1 Samuel 15:29 And also the Strength of Israel will not lie nor repent: for he is not a man, that he should repent.

*Hebrews 6:18 That by two immutable things, in which it was impossible for God to lie, we might have a strong consolation, who have fled for refuge to lay hold upon the hope set before us:

*Isaiah 45:5 I am the Lord, and there is none else, there is no God beside me: I girded thee, though thou hast not known me:6 That they may know from the rising of the sun, and from the west, that there is none beside me. I am the Lord, and there is none else.

*Isaiah 41:13 For I the Lord thy God will hold thy right hand, saying unto thee, Fear not; I will help thee.

*Psalm 78:38 But he, being full of compassion, forgave their iniquity, and destroyed them not: yea, many a time turned he his anger away, and did not stir up all his wrath.

Jesus Christ

In Hebrews 1 it is revealed that God had spoken to the fathers by the prophets, but has now spoken to us by his son Jesus Christ. According to ***Ephesians chapter 2:20 the kingdom of God is built upon the apostles and prophets, Jesus Christ himself being the chief cornerstone.*** Please notice that in times past God spoke specifically by the prophets to the father's, now we have a more sure word of prophecy, a deeper revelation, a more precise understanding of the perfect will of our heavenly Father. Why? Because he's going to speak to us in a very clear and dramatic way. If we will believe the words, the life, and the example of Jesus, it will radically transform our lives forever. The very 1st reality that will build an unmovable foundation in our hearts is the life of Jesus, the works of Jesus, the words of Jesus, the attitude of Jesus and the conduct of Jesus!

Remember all the words that had been spoken up to the coming of Christ were to prepare us for the coming of Christ. The life of Jesus is the perfect will of God manifested in the flesh. This is the mystery which had been hidden before the foundation of the world. Notice Hebrews 1: in verse 2 *hath in these last days spoken unto us by his Son!* The foundation of my understanding of the voice of God, the will of God, the purposes of God, the plan of God, the mission of God, the mysteries of God cannot be discovered in any greater revelation than the person of Jesus Christ! **There is no greater revelation of God's perfect divine will or voice then that which we discover in Jesus Christ.** I cannot emphasize this enough!

*Hebrews 1:1 God, who at sundry times and in divers manners spake in time past unto the fathers by the prophets, 2 hath in these last days spoken unto us by his Son, whom he hath appointed heir of all things, by whom also he made the worlds; 3 who being the brightness of his glory, and the express image of his person, and upholding all things by the word of his power, when he had by himself purged our sins, sat down on the right hand of the Majesty on high;

---

*John 1:14 And the Word was made flesh, and dwelt among us, (and we beheld his glory, the glory as of the only begotten of the Father,) full of grace and truth.

---

*John 14:9 Jesus saith unto him, have I been so long time with you, and yet hast thou not known me, Philip? He that hath seen me hath seen the Father; and how sayest thou then, Shew us the Father? 10 Believest thou not that I am in the Father, and the Father in me? The words that I speak unto you I speak not of myself: but the Father that dwelleth in me, he doeth the works

---

*Philippians 2:5 Let this mind be in you, which was also in Christ Jesus: 6 who, being in the form of God, thought it not robbery to be equal with God: 7 but made himself of no reputation, and took upon him the form of a servant, and was made in the likeness of men: 8 and being found in fashion as a man, he humbled himself, and became obedient unto death, even the death of the cross. 9 Wherefore God also hath highly exalted him, and given

him a name which is above every name: 10 that at the name of Jesus every knee should bow, of things in heaven, and things in earth, and things under the earth; 11 and that every tongue should confess that Jesus Christ is Lord, to the glory of God the Father.

---

*John 1:1 In the beginning was the Word, and the Word was with God, and the Word was God. 2 The same was in the beginning with God. 3 All things were made by him; and without him was not anything made that was made.

---

*Hebrews 13:8, "Jesus Christ the same yesterday, and today, and forever."

---

*Isaiah 42:5 Thus saith God the Lord, he that created the heavens, and stretched them out; he that spread forth the earth, and that which cometh out of it; he that giveth breath unto the people upon it, and spirit to them that walk therein:6 I the Lord have called thee in righteousness, and will hold thine hand, and will keep thee, and give thee for a covenant of the people, for a light of the Gentiles;7 To open the blind eyes, to bring out the prisoners from the prison, and them that sit in darkness out of the prison house.

---

*1 Corinthians 8:6 But to us there is but one God, the Father, of whom are all things, and we in him; and one Lord Jesus Christ, by whom are all things, and we by him.

---

*John 1:3 All things were made by him; and without him was not any thing made that was made.

---

*Matthew 28:18 And Jesus came and spake unto them, saying, All power is given unto me in heaven and in earth.

---

*1 Peter 1:20 Who verily was foreordained before the foundation of the world, but was manifest in these last times for you,

---

*John 3:16 For God so loved the world, that he gave his only begotten Son, that whosoever believeth in him should not perish, but have everlasting life.

---

*John 13:3 Jesus knowing that the Father had given all things into his hands, and that he was come from God, and went to God;

*John 1:17 For the law was given by Moses, but grace and truth came by Jesus Christ.18 No man hath seen God at any time, the only begotten Son, which is in the bosom of the Father, he hath declared him.

*Matthew 17:5 While he yet spake, behold, a bright cloud overshadowed them: and behold a voice out of the cloud, which said, This is my beloved Son, in whom I am well pleased; hear ye him.

*Hebrews 2:8 Thou hast put all things in subjection under his feet. For in that he put all in subjection under him, he left nothing that is not put under him. But now we see not yet all things put under him.9 But we see Jesus, who was made a little lower than the angels for the suffering of death, crowned with glory and honour; that he by the grace of God should taste death for every man.

*Hebrews 1:8 But unto the Son he saith, Thy throne, O God, is for ever and ever: a sceptre of righteousness is the sceptre of thy kingdom.*Hebrews 1:5 For unto which of the angels said he at any time, Thou art my Son, this day have I begotten thee? And again, I will be to him a Father, and he shall be to me a Son?

*Philippians 2:9 Wherefore God also hath highly exalted him, and given him a name which is above every name:10 That at the name of Jesus every knee should bow, of things in heaven, and things in earth, and things under the earth;11 And that every tongue should confess that Jesus Christ is Lord, to the glory of God the Father.

*Romans 1:4 And declared to be the Son of God with power, according to the spirit of holiness, by the resurrection from the dead:

*John 6:53 Then Jesus said unto them, Verily, verily, I say unto you, Except ye eat the flesh of the Son of man, and drink his blood, ye have no life in you.

*John 6:54 Whoso eateth my flesh, and drinketh my blood, hath eternal life; and I will raise him up at the last day.

*John 6:56 He that eateth my flesh, and drinketh my blood, dwelleth in me, and I in him.

Understanding Your Enemy

The satanic world is composed of demonic spirits who were formerly angels, and disembodied creatures who followed Lucifer in his rebellious treason against God. The very fiber of their moral character has been totally perverted and demoralized. There remains not even a sliver or spark of repentance. There is no love, mercy, sympathy, or kindness in their bosoms. They are murderers, liars, blasphemers, haters of mankind, propagators of the most horrible and outrageous crimes against creation, against man and God.

Many of the fallen angels appear to men as angels of light, so-called "guardians of mystical secrets." They sell their wares to gullible, money-seeking, self-gratifying, power-hungry humans. They appear in many forms promising immortality and limitless authority. They tote lies as the truth, declaring new revelations and higher realms of enlightenment. They push karma and New-Age theologies that deceive men and who have in turn deceived others. Even as the father of lies appeared to Adam and his wife in the garden of Eden, so they follow after the same pattern, promising that which they cannot give because they do not possess it. By their deceptions and perversions, they capture their prey as a spider captures a fly in its web, spinning a cocoon of lies around about their minds and emotions and slowly but surely injecting the deadly venom in order to possess and devour them. Much of their deceptions are woven with biblical truths and principles taken out of context.

They teach a Christianity that uses God, instead of one that surrenders its will and life to God. In the garden, Satan told Eve that she could eat of the Tree of the Knowledge of good and evil and not die. In the same way, the lie is still being propagated today to the masses of gullible people that we can continue to partake of good and evil and still live and not die. It is a lie that we can be like God and keep living in willful rebellion and disobedience. But true Christianity that brings salvation seeks the perfect will of God and reflects a life that hungers and thirsts after true holiness and righteousness.

These fallen angelic beings have only one purpose of existence, and that is to totally destroy anyone or anything that resembles the splendid nature of the glory of the Creator. They have fallen from their original glory and will never be able to ascend again to that magnificent position. For there is no repentance, nor forgiveness, nor redemption for these pitiful, lowly, corrupted beings that are destined to everlasting torment and damnation in the lake of fire, where the fire is never quenched, and the worm never dies.

Many have given heed to their seductive and damnable heresies, refusing to obey God and to turn from their wicked ways. Instead, they reach and strive for that forbidden fruit that even Lucifer grasped for in order to become God, which is the impossible, unattainable, and corrupted dream. For that which is created can never become greater or equal to the One who created him. It is like a gnat endeavoring to become an eagle or the clay pot longing to become the potter. Even as Lucifer lusted after God's power, position, anointing and authority, many today who have been deceived into believing that they are Christians are hungering and lusting after the exact same things. In truth, they should be longing for nothing but to be **just like Jesus in his character and nature**. Through Christ, God has given His sons and daughters the privilege to rule and reign with Him forever.

*John 8:44 Ye are of your father the devil, and the lusts of your father ye will do. He was a murderer from the beginning, and abode not in the truth, because there is no truth in him. When he speaketh a lie, he speaketh of his own: for he is a liar, and the father of it.

*John 10:10 The thief cometh not, but for to steal, and to kill, and to destroy: I am come that they might have life, and that they might have it more abundantly.

*Job 1:7 And the Lord said unto Satan, Whence comest thou? Then Satan answered the Lord, and said, From going to and fro in the earth, and from walking up and down in it.

*Job 2:7 So went Satan forth from the presence of the Lord, and smote Job with sore boils from the sole of his foot unto his crown.

*Acts 10:38 How God anointed Jesus of Nazareth with the Holy Ghost and with power: who went about doing good, and healing all that were oppressed of the devil; for God was with him.

*Psalm 106:37 Yea, they sacrificed their sons and their daughters unto devils,

*Ephesians 4:27 Neither give place to the devil.

*Ephesians 6:11 Put on the whole armour of God, that ye may be able to stand against the wiles of the devil.

*1 Timothy 4:1 Now the Spirit speaketh expressly, that in the latter times some shall depart from the faith, giving heed to seducing spirits, and doctrines of devils;

*2 Timothy 2:26 And that they may recover themselves out of the snare of the devil, who are taken captive by him at his will.

*Hebrews 2:14 Forasmuch then as the children are partakers of flesh and blood, he also himself likewise took part of the same; that through death he might destroy him that had the power of death, that is, the devil;

*James 2:19 Thou believest that there is one God; thou doest well: the devils also believe, and tremble.

*James 3:15 This wisdom descendeth not from above, but is earthly, sensual, devilish.16 For where envying and strife is, there is confusion and every evil work.

*James 4:7 Submit yourselves therefore to God. Resist the devil, and he will flee from you.

*1 Peter 5:8 Be sober, be vigilant; because your adversary the devil, as a roaring lion, walketh about, seeking whom he may devour:

1 John 3:8 He that committeth sin is of the devil; for the devil sinneth from the beginning. For this purpose the Son of God was manifested, that he might destroy the works of the devil.

*Revelation 12:9 And the great dragon was cast out, that old serpent, called the Devil, and Satan, which deceiveth the whole world: he was cast out into the earth, and his angels were cast out with him.

*Revelation 20:10 And the devil that deceived them was cast into the lake of fire and brimstone, where the beast and the false prophet are, and shall be tormented day and night for ever and ever.

We Are Soldiers

Our Confession as Gods Soldiers: I am a soldier in the army of my God, and the Lord Jesus Christ is my Commanding Officer. The Holy Scripture is my code of conduct, and many are the weapons of my warfare. I have been taught by the Holy Spirit, the fivefold ministry gifts, and trained by experience, tried by adversity, and tested in the fire.

I am a volunteer in this amazing army, and I am enlisted to my last breath. I will not get out, sell out, be talked out, or pushed out. I will strive to be faithful, reliable, capable and dependable. When God needs me, I am there. I am a soldier, and not a baby, and I do not need to be pampered, petted, primed up, pumped up, picked up, or pepped up. I am a soldier, and no one has to call me, remind me, write me, visit me, entice me, or lure me. I am a soldier, and I am not a wimp. I am in my proper place, saluting my King, obeying His orders, praising His name, and building His kingdom! No one has to send me flowers, gifts, food, cards or candy, or give me handouts. I do not need to be cuddled, cradled, cared for or catered to. I am committed, and I will not have my feelings hurt enough to turn me around. I cannot be discouraged to the point of turn me aside, and I cannot lose enough to cause me to ever quit.

When Jesus called me into this army, I had nothing to offer Him but my sinful life. If I end up with nothing, I will still come out ahead, and I will win. My God has and will continue to supply all of my needs according to His riches in glory. I am more than a conqueror, and I will always triumph in every situation. I can do all things through Christ who strengthens me. The devil will not defeat me, and people cannot disillusion me. Weather cannot weary me, and sickness will not stop me. Battles will not beat me, and money cannot buy me. Governments will not silence me, and hell cannot deny me. I am a soldier for Christ even unto death. I am a soldier in the army of God, and I am marching to the song of the Redeemed. I am a soldier, marching towards heaven with every step! *(doc yeager, plus unknown Author)*

*Revelation 19:11 And I saw heaven opened, and behold a white horse; and he that sat upon him was called Faithful and True, and in righteousness he doth judge and make war.12 His eyes were as a flame of fire, and on his head were many crowns; and he had a name written, that no man knew, but he himself.13 And he was clothed with a vesture dipped in blood: and his name is called The Word of God.14 And the armies which were in heaven followed him upon white horses, clothed in fine linen, white and clean.15 And out of his mouth goeth a sharp sword, that with it he should smite the nations: and he shall rule them with a rod of iron: and he treadeth the winepress of the

fierceness and wrath of Almighty God.16 And he hath on his vesture and on his thigh a name written, King Of Kings, And Lord Of Lords.

---

*Exodus 15:3 The Lord is a man of war: the Lord is his name.

---

*Isaiah 42:13 The Lord shall go forth as a mighty man, he shall stir up jealousy like a man of war: he shall cry, yea, roar; he shall prevail against his enemies.

---

*Joshua 5:14 And he said, Nay; but as captain of the host of the Lord am I now come.

---

*Psalm 24:8 Who is this King of glory? The Lord strong and mighty, the Lord mighty in battle.

---

*Colossians 2:15 And having spoiled principalities and powers, he made a shew of them openly, triumphing over them in it.

---

*Psalm 45:3 Gird thy sword upon thy thigh, O most mighty, with thy glory and thy majesty.4 And in thy majesty ride prosperously because of truth and meekness and righteousness; and thy right hand shall teach thee terrible things.5 Thine arrows are sharp in the heart of the king's enemies; whereby the people fall under thee.6 Thy throne, O God, is for ever and ever: the sceptre of thy kingdom is a right sceptre.

---

*Isaiah 9:6 For unto us a child is born, unto us a son is given: and the government shall be upon his shoulder: and his name shall be called Wonderful, Counsellor, The mighty God, The everlasting Father, The Prince of Peace.

---

*2 Timothy 2:3 Thou therefore endure hardness, as a good soldier of Jesus Christ.

---

*2 Timothy 2:4 No man that warreth entangleth himself with the affairs of this life; that he may please him who hath chosen him to be a soldier.

---

*Isaiah 9:5 For every battle of the warrior is with confused noise, and garments rolled in blood; but this shall be with burning and fuel of fire.

CHAPTER TWO

The Believers Armor

Battle Armor is revealed to us for the first time in the book of Judges 9. The first time the Bible talks about there being war is in Genesis 14. In Genesis 3:24 it talks about God placing a flaming sword at the entrance of the garden of Eden to keep man out. In first Samuel 17 it talks about Goliaths helmet. The point I'm trying to make is that from the very beginning there has been **armor** and **weapons** used in the **midst of warfare**. We are in a war whether we like it or not. God has provided for us **armor** and **weapons** that we must use against the enemy. Actually every **promise** that God has provided in the Scriptures (**over 7000 promises**) have been given to us in order to defeat our enemy, and in succeeding in God's perfect will. It is by the **armor of God's promises** that we are guaranteed our victory against every work of the enemy. Let us first look at the Scriptures that talk about the **armor**.

*Romans 13:12 The night is far spent, the day is at hand: let us therefore cast off the works of darkness, and let us put on the armour of light.

*2 Corinthians 6:7 By the word of truth, by the power of God, by the armour of righteousness on the right hand and on the left,

*Ephesians 6:11 Put on the whole armour of God, that ye may be able to stand against the wiles of the devil.

*Ephesians 6:13 Wherefore take unto you the whole armour of God, that ye may be able to withstand in the evil day, and having done all, to stand.

*2 Corinthians 10:4 (For the weapons of our warfare are not carnal, but mighty through God to the pulling down of strong holds;)

*1 Thessalonians 5:8 But let us, who are of the day, be sober, putting on the breastplate of faith and love; and for an helmet, the hope of salvation.

Overcoming By God's Promises

I cannot emphasize enough the importance of God's promises. Over 7000 promises are given to those who cry out to God for forgiveness, mercy, and help. These promises are God's surety of his response to those who look to him. Based upon these promises we are able to overcome every attack, and affliction of the devil with his demonic horde. By these promises we become partakers of the divine nature of God the Father, Jesus Christ, and the Holy Ghost. Many of these promises have conditions that must be met, If's revealed to us in the word of God.

*2 Chronicles 7:14 If my people, which are called by my name, shall humble themselves, and pray, and seek my face, and turn from their wicked ways; then will I hear from heaven, and will forgive their sin, and will heal their land.

By these exceeding great, and precious promises we have a foundation that we can build our life upon. By these promises we are building upon a the Rock Christ Jesus that the storms of life will not be able to overcome or be able to defeat us. It is not sufficient for us just to know that these promises are available, but we must take advantage of every one of them, hiding them in our hearts. We must act upon these realities, these truths, these powerful promises that God has given to each one of us.

*2 Peter 1:4 Whereby are given unto us exceeding great and precious promises: that by these ye might be partakers of the divine nature, having escaped the corruption that is in the world through lust.

*1 John 2:25 And this is the promise that he hath promised us, even eternal life.

*Titus 1:2 In hope of eternal life, which God, that cannot lie, promised before the world began;

*2 Corinthians 1:20 For all the promises of God in him are yea, and in him Amen, unto the glory of God by us.

*2 Corinthians 7:1 Having therefore these promises, dearly beloved, let us cleanse ourselves from all filthiness of the flesh and spirit, perfecting holiness in the fear of God.

*2 Peter 3:9 The Lord is not slack concerning his promise, as some men count slackness; but is longsuffering to us-ward, not willing that any should perish, but that all should come to repentance.

*2 Peter 3:13 Nevertheless we, according to his promise, look for new heavens and a new earth, wherein dwelleth righteousness.

*Luke 24:49 And, behold, I send the promise of my Father upon you: but tarry ye in the city of Jerusalem, until ye be endued with power from on high.

*Ephesians 1:13 In whom ye also trusted, after that ye heard the word of truth, the gospel of your salvation: in whom also after that ye believed, ye were sealed with that holy Spirit of promise,

*Galatians 3:16 Now to Abraham and his seed were the promises made. He saith not, And to seeds, as of many; but as of one, And to thy seed, which is Christ.

*Galatians 3:29 And if ye be Christ's, then are ye Abraham's seed, and heirs according to the promise.

*1 Timothy 4:8 For bodily exercise profiteth little: but godliness is profitable unto all things, having promise of the life that now is, and of that which is to come.

*Hebrews 4:1 Let us therefore fear, lest, a promise being left us of entering into his rest, any of you should seem to come short of it.

*Hebrews 6:12 That ye be not slothful, but followers of them who through faith and patience inherit the promises.

*Hebrews 6:17 Wherein God, willing more abundantly to shew unto the heirs of promise the immutability of his counsel, confirmed it by an oath: 18 That by two immutable things, in which it was impossible for God to lie, we might have a strong consolation, who have fled for refuge to lay hold upon the hope set before us:

*Hebrews 10:36 For ye have need of patience, that, after ye have done the will of God, ye might receive the promise.

*Hebrews 11:33 Who through faith subdued kingdoms, wrought righteousness, obtained promises, stopped the mouths of lions.

*James 1:12 Blessed is the man that endureth temptation: for when he is tried, he shall receive the crown of life, which the Lord hath promised to them that love him.

*James 2:5 Hearken, my beloved brethren, Hath not God chosen the poor of this world rich in faith, and heirs of the kingdom which he hath promised to them that love him?

Weapons Of War

The Written Word, the Bible equals the absolute will of God. The weapons that God has made available to us is all through, by, and in his word. The word of God is also the voice of God, and it must become more real to you than anything else in this world. Believers tell me all the time that God does not speak to them, but they are sadly mistaken. He speaks to us through the holy book called the Bible.

*2 Timothy 3:16 All scripture is given by inspiration of God, and is profitable for doctrine, for reproof, for correction, for instruction in righteousness:

God speaks to us is through the written word. Remember that Christ, His Life and His words are the major way and foundation that as believers we must build our life upon. This is an order for us to be fully equipped and armored to overcome the world, the flesh, and the devil! Only when the truth of God's word that has been spoken and reviewed to us through Christ (established in our hearts), can we go to all of the written word, the epistles, and the Old Testament with understanding. What must take priority over all Scripture is what Jesus said and did. After this reality then we can go to the epistles of Paul, Peter, Philip, James, the book of Jude, and all of the WORD with divine and clear understanding.

*Isaiah 54:17 No weapon that is formed against thee shall prosper; and every tongue that shall rise against thee in judgment thou shalt condemn. This is the heritage of the servants of the Lord, and their righteousness is of me, saith the Lord.

*Jeremiah 51:20 Thou art my battle axe and weapons of war: for with thee will I break in pieces the nations, and with thee will I destroy kingdoms;
*2 Corinthians 10:4 (For the weapons of our warfare are not carnal, but mighty through God to the pulling down of strong holds;)

*Luke 4:32 And they were astonished at his doctrine: for his word was with power.

*Hebrews 1:3 Who being the brightness of his glory, and the express image of his person, and upholding all things by the word of his power, when he had by himself purged our sins, sat down on the right hand of the Majesty on high:

*Hebrews 4:12 For the word of God is quick, and powerful, and sharper than any twoedged sword, piercing even to the dividing asunder of soul and spirit, and of the joints and marrow, and is a discerner of the thoughts and intents of the heart.

*Psalm 33:6 By the word of the Lord were the heavens made; and all the host of them by the breath of his mouth.

*Psalm 119:89 Forever, O Lord, thy word is settled in heaven.
*Matthew 24:35 Heaven and earth shall pass away, but my words shall not pass away.

*2 Peter 3:7 But the heavens and the earth, which are now, by the same word are kept in store, reserved unto fire against the day of judgment and perdition of ungodly men.

*1 John 5:7 For there are three that bear record in heaven, the Father, the Word, and the Holy Ghost: and these three are one.
*Psalm 107:20 He sent his word, and healed them, and delivered them from their destructions.

*Psalm 147:15 He sendeth forth his commandment upon earth: his word runneth very swiftly.

*Isaiah 55:11 So shall my word be that goeth forth out of my mouth: it shall not return unto me void, but it shall accomplish that which I please, and it shall prosper in the thing whereto I sent it.

*John 6:63 It is the spirit that quickeneth; the flesh profiteth nothing: the words that I speak unto you, they are spirit, and they are life.

*Isaiah 45:23 I have sworn by myself, the word is gone out of my mouth in righteousness, and shall not return, That unto me every knee shall bow, every tongue shall swear.

*Romans 10:17 So then faith cometh by hearing, and hearing by the word of God.

*1 Peter 1:23 Being born again, not of corruptible seed, but of incorruptible, by the word of God, which liveth and abideth for ever.

*James 1:18 Of his own will begat he us with the word of truth, that we should be a kind of firstfruits of his creatures.

*Jeremiah 1:10 See, I have this day set thee over the nations and over the kingdoms, to root out, and to pull down, and to destroy, and to throw down, to build, and to plant. (with Gods Word)

We Must Meditate

On this particle area we will go into much greater detail. Understand that your meditation and how much you meditate on Gods (word) Promises will determine your victory over the devil, and the flesh! There must be a transformation in your thinking processes by the means of meditation on God's WORD. You have to take your head and your heart and give them completely to God. I mean all of who you are, needs to be given to God.

*Isaiah 26:3 Thou wilt keep him in perfect peace, whose mind is stayed on thee: because he trusteth in thee.

---

*Proverbs 3:5 Trust in the LORD with all thine heart; and lean not unto thine own understanding.6 In all thy ways acknowledge him, and he shall direct thy paths.

The Scriptures declare that if **two be not agreed together, they cannot walk together**. Faith is when you come into complete agreement with God, his Word, and his will. Paul said by the spirit of God, be not conformed to this world, but be ye transformed (**metamorphosis**) this means being changed by the renewing of our mind.

Before your mind is transformed, renewed we are like a **caterpillar**. The number of legs and feet that a **caterpillar** has varies. There is one type of caterpillar that has 16 legs, and 16 feet, which they use to hold on to anything, and everything they can. When that **caterpillar** becomes a **Butterfly**, everything changes. Including the number of feet they have, and their purpose. All Butterflies end up with SIX legs and feet. In some species such as the monarch, the front pair of legs remains tucked up under the body most of the time. Their legs become long and slender, and something amazing happens to their feet, because within their feet are now taste buds. That means that whatever their feet touch they taste. It prevents them from eating anything that is not good for them. When they were **caterpillars** they were willing to eat everything their little feet took a hold of. You see the **Butterfly** which came from the caterpillar now lives in a completely different world. It is no longer bound by earthly things. It no longer has feet that cling to the Earth! It is free to fly above all the worries, fears, anxieties, enemies, and circumstances of life. It literally can see into the future, where it is going. It has overcome the law of gravitation, by a superior law. It is called the law of aerodynamics. We as believers, as we renew our minds leave behind the law of sin and death, entering into a new world called: **The Law of the Spirit of Life in Christ Jesus**! We need to be very picky at what we eat mentally. Whatever we place in our minds and our hearts, is what we will meditate upon. As *a man thinketh, so is he!*

Romans 8:2 For the law of the Spirit of life in Christ Jesus hath made me free from the law of sin and death.

To operate in God's kingdom, you **MUST renew your mind**. Your walk with God cannot be higher than that of the **renewing of your mind**. Everything that is contradictory to the word, the will, the divine nature of **Jesus Christ** must be dealt with. As we bring every thought captive to the obedience of **Christ**, we will begin soar like an eagle. Listen to what James the brother of **Jesus** said about the renewing of the mind.

*James 1:21 Wherefore lay apart all filthiness and superfluity of naughtiness, and receive with meekness the engrafted word, which is able to save your souls.

WE CAN NOT BE DEFEATED WHEN WE ARE LIVING, WALKING & MOVING WITH A RENEWED MIND!

There are so many Scriptures dealing with the renewing of your mind, by the **meditation** of God's Word in your heart, that many books could be written on this subject. I will share with you only a small number of Scriptures that are important to this particular subject. Then I will share with you how you meditate.

*Joshua 1:8 This book of the law shall not depart out of thy mouth; but thou shalt meditate therein day and night, that thou mayest observe to do according to all that is written therein: for then thou shalt make thy way prosperous, and then thou shalt have good success.

*Psalm 1:2 But his delight is in the law of the Lord; and in his law doth he meditate day and night.

*Psalm 63:6 when I remember thee upon my bed, and meditate on thee in the night watches.

*Psalm 77:12 I will meditate also of all thy work, and talk of thy doings.

*Psalm 119:148 Mine eyes prevent the night watches, that I might meditate in thy word.

*Psalm 104:34 My meditation of him shall be sweet: I will be glad in the Lord.

*Psalm 119:97 O how love I thy law! it is my meditation all the day.

*Psalm 119:99 I have more understanding than all my teachers: for thy testimonies are my meditation.

*1Timothy 4:15 Meditate upon these things; give thyself wholly to them; that thy profiting may appear to all.

*Psalm 39:3 My heart was hot within me, while I was musing the fire burned: then spake I with my tongue,

*2Samuel 23:2 The Spirit of the Lord spake by me, and his word was in my tongue.

What Is Meditation?

To meditate means to Muse, to Ponder, to Think Upon, To Mutter, Recite, To Talk to Yourself. It is way more than just memorization. In the most basic form it would be what we call to worry, but it's the opposite of worry. When you worry about something, it is like a record stuck in a groove that keeps playing over and over. Have you ever had a song that just would not leave your mind? You sang it to yourself in your mind, and even with your lips, because it got into your head, and your heart. This is what meditation is. We need to meditate upon the word, the will, the personality of **Jesus Christ** day and night. This will bring about a wonderful transformation.

In nature God has given to us many examples that can be applied to spiritually. I think one of the greatest examples of meditation is revealed to us through the process of dairy cows, turning green grass into wonderful white and creamy milk.

How do Cows Make Milk?

Or we could say:

How do Believers Grow in Faith?

#1 First A cow only starts to produce milk once her first calf is born.

(Even so we must become impregnated by the word of God, being born again by the spirit and the water, in order to walk where Jesus walked)

#2 A cow will only produces milk for as long as she keeps eating massive amounts of living green grass, chewing the cud, and is milked. If any of these processes are stopped, she will stop producing milk.

(The believer must keep eating the living word of God, chewing it, and then doing it! Doing it would equal that of the dairy cow being milked!)

***John 6:53 Then Jesus said unto them, Verily, verily, I say unto you, Except ye eat the flesh of the Son of man, and drink his blood, ye have no life in you. 54 Whoso eateth my flesh, and drinketh my blood, hath eternal life; and I will raise him up at the last day. 55 For my flesh is meat indeed, and my blood is drink indeed.**

#3 Cows belong to a group of animals called ruminants. All of these animals have **four stomach compartments,** and each compartment has a specific part in digesting food. [Amazingly sheep are included in this animal group.] The transformation of grass into milk is not instantaneous, or accomplished quickly. It will take about **70 hours** for a cow to turn grass into milk!

(Even so is it with faith. As you begin to meditate upon the word consistently hour after hour, day after day, faith will begin to be produced in your heart and your life! Many believers do not have this understanding. They chew a little bit of the word, for a little bit of time, and then are disappointed when faith dose not pour out of their hearts like a mighty river)

#4 Blood has a significant part of the cow producing milk. For every **2 to 3 cups of milk** a cow makes, more than **105 gallons** of blood must travel around her udder to deliver the nutrients and water for making milk. In total a cow has about **12 gallons** of blood in her body, so her blood is always **on the move** around the udder to keep making milk.

Even so with the believer, there must be continual moving of the Holy Spirit in our lives for us to produce faith. This is why Jesus asked: will there be any faith left on the earth when he returns? It is because there is very little moving of the spirit in many church gatherings today, much less in a believer's everyday life. And yet in Ephesians it tells us to be filled with the spirit beginning in chapter 5 verse 17. It will take massive amounts of the word and the moving of the spirit to produce the faith that is necessary to live the same life that Jesus did!

#5 To produce milk, cows must eat a variety of grasses, clover and bulky fodder, which make them feel full, plus food rich in protein and energy. If the pasture (**pastor**) they are eating from is not providing the right kind of foods, it will cause the cow to produce dismal results. It only takes the cow to be eating one wrong type of vegetation for it to ruin its milk. And it can have dire consequences to the health of the cow. It could even die!

(Even so is it with the believer. If the pastor (pasture) is not providing healthy, spiritual truths, preaching the reality of Jesus Christ, His will and His purposes, it will not produce faith that prevails and overcomes the obstacles of life)

Now let us look at the four stomach compartments (digestive compartments) and their special functions:

The stomach: The heart of man, his mind, will, emotions, attitude, disposition, purpose for living could be likened unto the cows stomach.

1. The rumen

When cows graze on grass they swallow the grass half-chewed and mix it with water in their first stomach - the rumen - which can hold about **13 gallons** of chewed grass. It is here that the digestive process begins. The rumen softens and breaks down the grass with stomach juices and microbes (or bacteria).

(Even so with the believer, we begin to hide Scriptures within our heart. We memorize these Scriptures. This is the first process. The Holy Spirit can do very little with the Scriptures unto they are memorized)

2. The reticulum

In the reticulum the grass is made even softer and is formed into small wads called cuds. Each cud is then returned to the mouth where the cow chews it **40 to 60** times (for about one minute). Each card is chewed for almost an hour!

(After the believer has memorized the Scripture it now must be spoken (chewed) for at least an hour. Within this time frame the Holy Spirit begins to change the word of God from letter into spirit.)

3. The omasum

The chewed cud is swallowed into the third stomach, the omasum, where it is pressed to remove water and broken down further.

(This is where things really begin to get interesting, because now the word begins to be assimilated into your heart. It begins to take upon it a reality that you have never known. It begins to renew and transform your mind).

King David said: **My heart was hot within me, while I was musing the fire burned: then spake I with my tongue,**

4. The abomasum

The grass then passes to the fourth stomach, called the abomasum, where it is digested. The digested grass then passes through the small intestine, where all the essential nutrients the cow needs to stay healthy and strong are absorbed, and some are transported to the udder.

(Life is now beginning to flood the believer. Divine wisdom and strength is beginning to overtake him or her. The reality of Christ is exploding in their minds, their thoughts, their deeds, and their actions. Even as the milk comes forth from the utter of the cow, so now the works of the kingdom are being produced through our lives. People are beginning to see, hear, and experience Jesus Christ in and through us!)

The Holy Ghost

I could never over emphasize the importance of the baptism of the Holy Ghost. Christ himself did not begin his earthly ministry in ministering to the multitudes until after he received the Holy Ghost at the river Jordan. We are dealing with supernatural enemies, and we need a supernatural endowment in order to overcome these enemies. When we believe and receive the Holy Ghost, there is placed within us a power greater than all of the combined forces of hell itself.

*1 John 4:4 Ye are of God, little children, and have overcome them: because greater is he that is in you, than he that is in the world.

The Holy Ghost will take the word and breathe life into it, causing the letter of the word to be turned into spirit. In order for the Holy Spirit to do this, we must be in complete agreement with the Bible. You do not need to understand the Scriptures in order to agree with them. Simply boldly declared to yourself, I agree with the Bible, no matter what it says. Every dream, vision, healing, miracle, supernatural experience is a quickening of the Holy Ghost. This quickening is revealed to us in the book of Romans when God spoke to the heart of Abraham.

*Romans 4:17 (As it is written, I have made thee a father of many nations,) before him whom he believed, even God, who quickeneth the dead, and calleth those things which be not as though they were.

God had to Quicken us in order for us to be born again, in order for us to be drawn to God.

*John 6:44 No man can come to me, except the Father which hath sent me draw him: and I will raise him up at the last day.

The quickening of the Holy Ghost makes all the difference between victory and defeat. Now you could have heard the gospel for your whole life, and yet not be convicted or touched by the spirit of God in the least. The word of God was just sliding off of your back like water off of the back of a duck. Then all of a sudden one day out of the blue everything changed. The spirit of God quickened your heart in such a dramatic way that it felt like God was reaching into your chest and squeezing your heart. You fell under tremendous and overwhelming conviction, with everything inside of you crying out to be right with God. This is the quickening, convicting power of the Holy Spirit that will wonderfully change and transform you. This quickening is not just for the salvation of our souls, but it is a major way in which God will lead us, and guide us. Many times the messages that the Lord has me preach is because of the quickening of the Holy Ghost in my heart. God will Quicken certain Scriptures to my heart throughout the week as I get ready to minister my message on Sunday. This is the spirit of God leading and guiding me by his quickening. The spirit of God will Quicken your heart throughout the day, as you walk moment by moment.

*John 16:7 Nevertheless I tell you the truth; It is expedient for you that I go away: for if I go not away, the Comforter will not come unto you; but if I depart, I will send him unto you.

---

*Luke 4:18 The Spirit of the Lord is upon me, because he hath anointed me to preach the gospel to the poor; he hath sent me to heal the brokenhearted, to preach deliverance to the captives, and recovering of sight to the blind, to set at liberty them that are bruised,19 To preach the acceptable year of the Lord.

---

*Acts 10:38 How God anointed Jesus of Nazareth with the Holy Ghost and with power: who went about doing good, and healing all that were oppressed of the devil; for God was with him.

---

*2 Corinthians 3:17 Now the Lord is that Spirit: and where the Spirit of the Lord is, there is liberty.

---

*2 Corinthians 3:6 Who also hath made us able ministers of the new testament; not of the letter, but of the spirit: for the letter killeth, but the spirit giveth life.

---

*Luke 24:49 And, behold, I send the promise of my Father upon you: but tarry ye in the city of Jerusalem, until ye be endued with power from on high.

---

*Acts 1:8 But ye shall receive power, after that the Holy Ghost is come upon you: and ye shall be witnesses unto me both in Jerusalem, and in all Judaea, and in Samaria, and unto the uttermost part of the earth.

---

*Joel 2:28 And it shall come to pass afterward, that I will pour out my spirit upon all flesh; and your sons and your daughters shall prophesy, your old men shall dream dreams, your young men shall see visions:29 And also upon the servants and upon the handmaids in those days will I pour out my spirit.

---

*John 14:26 But the Comforter, which is the Holy Ghost, whom the Father will send in my name, he shall teach you all things, and bring all things to your remembrance, whatsoever I have said unto you.

---

*John 15:26 But when the Comforter is come, whom I will send unto you from the Father, even the Spirit of truth, which proceedeth from the Father, he shall testify of me:

---

*John 16:7 Nevertheless I tell you the truth; It is expedient for you that I go away: for if I go not away, the Comforter will not come unto you; but if I depart, I will send him unto you.

---

*Isaiah 59:21 As for me, this is my covenant with them, saith the Lord; My spirit that is upon thee, and my words which I have put in thy mouth, shall not depart out of thy mouth, nor out of the mouth of thy seed, nor out of the mouth of thy seed's seed, saith the Lord, from henceforth and forever.

---

*Isaiah 44:3 For I will pour water upon him that is thirsty, and floods upon the dry ground: I will pour my spirit upon thy seed, and my blessing upon thine offspring:

---

*John 14:16 And I will pray the Father, and he shall give you another Comforter, that he may abide with you forever;17 Even the Spirit of truth; whom the world cannot receive, because it seeth him not, neither knoweth him: but ye know him; for he dwelleth with you, and shall be in you.

---

*Zechariah 4:6 ....Not by might, nor by power, but by my spirit, saith the Lord of hosts.

---

*Romans 15:19 Through mighty signs and wonders, by the power of the Spirit of God; so that from Jerusalem, and round about unto Illyricum, I have fully preached the gospel of Christ.

---

*2 Corinthians 12:12 Truly the signs of an apostle were wrought among you in all patience, in signs, and wonders, and mighty deeds.

---

*Acts 4:33 And with great power gave the apostles witness of the resurrection of the Lord Jesus: and great grace was upon them all.
*Hebrews 2:4 God also bearing them witness, both with signs and wonders, and with divers miracles, and gifts of the Holy Ghost, according to his own will?

---

*1 Thessalonians 1:5 For our gospel came not unto you in word only, but also in power, and in the Holy Ghost, and in much assurance; as ye know what manner of men we were among you for your sake.

---

*Acts 5:12 And by the hands of the apostles were many signs and wonders wrought among the people; (and they were all with one accord in Solomon's porch.

---

*Acts 4:30 By stretching forth thine hand to heal; and that signs and wonders may be done by the name of thy holy child Jesus.31 And when they had prayed, the place was shaken where they were assembled together; and they were all filled with the Holy Ghost, and they spake the word of God with boldness.

---

*Romans 8:13 For if ye live after the flesh, ye shall die: but if ye through the Spirit do mortify the deeds of the body, ye shall live.

---

*Romans 8:13 For if ye live after the flesh, ye shall die: but if ye through the Spirit do mortify the deeds of the body, ye shall live.

Books Written by Doc Yeager:

"Living in the Realm of the Miraculous #1"

"I need God Cause I'm Stupid"

"The Miracles of Smith Wigglesworth"

"How Faith Comes 28 WAYS"

"Horrors of Hell, Splendors of Heaven"

"The Coming Great Awakening"

"Sinners In The Hands of an Angry GOD", "(modernized)"

"Brain Parasite Epidemic"

"My JOURNEY To HELL" - illustrated for teenagers

"Divine Revelation Of Jesus Christ"

"My Daily Meditations"

"Holy Bible of JESUS CHRIST"

"War In The Heavenlies - (Chronicles of Micah)"

"Living in the Realm of the Miraculous #2"

"My Legal Rights To Witness"

"Why We (MUST) Gather!- 30 Biblical Reasons"

"My Incredible, Supernatural, Divine Experiences"

"How GOD Leads & Guides! - 20 Ways"

"Living in the Realm of the Miraculous #3"

CHAPTER THREE

Looking At Our Armor

God has provided for the believer divine weapons, supernatural armor that we need to appropriate in order to overcome the enemy. These weapons are offensive and defensive in nature. In **Ephesians chapter 6**, Paul the apostle speaks about **seven** of these weapons used in our armor. I come from a long line of military family, and my family members throughout many generations have been involved in the Army, Navy, Air Force, Marines, and special forces. When I joined the Navy as a 17-year-old, it was in the Navy that I was employed. The very first thing that I went through was boot camp. In boot camp we were conditioned for battle mentally, physically, and emotionally. We had to learn how to take orders, and respond immediately. We also were trained in being a team, and being in unity. As we progressed physically, mentally and emotionally, they began to introduce us to different types of weapons. One of the first weapons that we were taught to use was an M-16.

Now that I am in the Lord's army, military, there are realities that I must learn. It does not come naturally, any more than when your mother gave birth to you, did you know how to automatically walk and talk. We have stepped into a new kingdom, with new principles, laws, attitudes and disciplines. We must be trained in how to walk, talk, live, fight and do battle with our enemy. In **Ephesians chapter 4** Paul the apostle reveals that when Christ ascended up on high, he gave gifts to the body of Christ for our perfection and maturity. This is the purpose of writing this book, in order to help us to become fully equipped, prepared, and ready to do battle. All of these weapons, and armor that God has provided is based upon the eternal truths given to us in the Bible.

*Ephesians 6:13 Wherefore take unto you the whole armour of God, that ye may be able to withstand in the evil day, and having done all, to stand.14 Stand therefore, having your <u>loins girt about with truth</u>, and having on the <u>breastplate of righteousness</u>;15 And your <u>feet shod with the preparation of the gospel of peace</u>;16 Above all, taking the <u>shield of faith</u>, wherewith ye shall be able to quench all the fiery darts of the wicked.17 And take the <u>helmet of salvation</u>, and the <u>sword of the Spirit</u>, which is the word of God:18 <u>Praying always with all prayer and supplication</u> in the Spirit, and watching thereunto with all perseverance and supplication for all saints;

Verse 13 - Wherefore - Because ye have such enemies to contend with, take unto you - as provided and prepared for you, the whole armor of God; which armor if you put on and use, you shall be both invulnerable and immortal. The ancient heroes are fabled to have had armor sent to them by the gods; and even the great armor-maker, Vulcan, was reputed to be a god himself. This was complete fable: What Paul speaks of is reality.

That ye may be able to withstand - That ye may not only stand fast in the liberty wherewith Christ hath made you free, but also overcome all your spiritual foes; and stay in your ranks, maintain your ground against them, never putting off your armor, but standing always ready prepared to repel any and all attacks.

And having done all, to stand - (Greek), And having conquered all, stand: this is a military phrase, and is repeatedly used in this form by the best Greek writers.

Loins Girt about with Truth

The first piece of God's armor is represented by the Roman soldier's **BELT**! Paul encourages believers to "fasten the belt of truth around their waist" (Eph. 6:14). This belt is **TRUTH**! Truth is our foundational, motto, principle, and attitude. The truth of God's Word is what we use to perceive Satan's lies. Our belt of Truth also protects our vital spiritual organs. Satan seeks to accuse us so that we will be disqualified from God's use. His lies and accusations attempt stop us from doing anything for Gods honor, but the truth of God's Word gives us the Victory in Christ.

This belt of Truth enables the believer to do battle. This belt is absolutely essential for the believer to battle successfully against every scheme of Satan. Without knowing biblical truth, we are subject to being "carried about by every wind of doctrine, by the trickery of men, by craftiness in deceitful scheming" (Ephesians 4:14). To be girded with truth reveals an attitude of readiness and of genuine commitment. It is the mark of the sincere believer who forsakes the darkness of this present evil age. Every aspect of life that might hinder our work for the Lord is gathered and tucked into our belt of truth so that it will be out of the way in the battle. Paul said, **2 Timothy 2:4 No man that warreth entangleth himself with the affairs of this life; that he may please him who hath chosen him to be a soldier.**

Being girded with truth is being renewed in your mind and proving "what the will of God is, that which is the good, the acceptable, and the perfect will of

God" (Romans 12:2). When you renew your mind by committing yourself to God's truth, you will become "a living and holy sacrifice, acceptable to God, prepared unto every good work, which is your spiritual duty.

*John 8:32 And ye shall know the truth, and the truth shall make you free.

_____

*John 1:17 For the law was given by Moses, but grace and truth came by Jesus Christ.

_____

*John 4:23 But the hour cometh, and now is, when the true worshippers shall worship the Father in spirit and in truth: for the Father seeketh such to worship him.

_____

*John 4:24 God is a Spirit: and they that worship him must worship him in spirit and in truth.

_____

*John 14:6 Jesus saith unto him, I am the way, the truth, and the life: no man cometh unto the Father, but by me.

_____

*John 17:17 Sanctify them through thy truth: thy word is truth.

_____

*1 Corinthians 13:6 Rejoiceth not in iniquity, but rejoiceth in the truth;

_____

*Ephesians 1:13 In whom ye also trusted, after that ye heard the word of truth, the gospel of your salvation:

_____

*Ephesians 5:9 (For the fruit of the Spirit is in all goodness and righteousness and truth;)

_____

*2 Thessalonians 2:12 That they all might be damned who believed not the truth, but had pleasure in unrighteousness.

_____

*1 Timothy 2:4 Who will have all men to be saved, and to come unto the knowledge of the truth.

_____

*2 Timothy 4:4 And they shall turn away their ears from the truth, and shall be turned unto fables.

*James 1:18 Of his own will begat he us with the word of truth, that we should be a kind of firstfruits of his creatures.

*1 John 2:4 He that saith, I know him, and keepeth not his commandments, is a liar, and the truth is not in him.

*1 John 1:8 If we say that we have no sin, we deceive ourselves, and the truth is not in us.

*1 John 1:6 If we say that we have fellowship with him, and walk in darkness, we lie, and do not the truth:

Breastplate Of Righteousness

The second piece of God's armor is represented by the Roman soldier's **Breastplate**. No Roman soldier would go into battle without his breastplate--a tough sleeveless piece of armor that covered everything apart from his head and limbs. It was often made of leather or heavy linen, onto which were sewn overlapping pieces of metal molded or hammered to conform to the body. The purpose of that piece of armor is obvious--to protect one's heart, lungs, intestines, and other vital organs.

Satan seeks to assault us at our very core. His whispers and accusations are aimed to corrupt the parts of our inner self to steal our identity and replace it with his perverted and twisted personality. The mind and the emotions are the two areas where Satan most fiercely attacks the believer. He wants to cloud our minds with false doctrine, false principles, and false information to mislead and confuse us. He also wants to confuse our emotions and thereby pervert our affection, morals, loyalties, goals, and commitments. He desires to snatch the Word of God from our hearts, our minds and our lives, in order to replace it with his own perverse ideas. He seeks to undermine pure living and replace it with immorality, greed, envy, hate, and every other evil vice. He wants us to laugh at sin rather than mourn over it, and to rationalize it rather than confess it, and to cause us not to turn away from it. He seduces us to become so accustomed to sin in us and around us that it no longer disturbs us.

Our protection against these attacks is the breastplate of righteousness. Divine Righteousness is to be taken and wrapped around our whole being, just as ancient soldiers covered themselves with armor breastplates. Paul here is obviously not speaking of self-righteousness, which is not righteousness at all but the sin of pride. Nor is he speaking of imputed righteousness--the righteousness God applies to the account of every Christian the moment he believes in Christ (Romans 4:6, 11, 22-24). **The breastplate of righteousness is the practical righteousness of moment-by-moment obedience to God's Word.**

This breastplate of righteousness is the genuine holiness of Christ that brings "every thought captive to the obedience of Christ" (2 Corinthians 10:5) and whose mind is set "on the things above, not on the things that are on earth" (Colossians 3:2). The Breast-Plate; consisted of two parts, one that coveres the whole region of the thorax or breast, in which the principal viscera of life are contained; and the other covered the back, as far down as the front part extended.

The breast-plate of righteousness - signifies the principle of righteousness; it signifies the practice of righteousness, or living a holy life; it signifies God's method of justifying sinners; and it signifies justification itself. The principle of righteousness or true holiness implanted in the heart by the new birth, the divine nature of God in us; a holy life, a life regulated according to the testimonies of God. As the breast-plate defends the heart and lungs, and all those vital functionaries that are contained in what is called the region of the thorax; so this righteousness, this life of God in the soul of man, defends every thing on which the man's spiritual existence depends. While he possesses this principle, and acts from it, his spiritual and eternal life is secure.

*Matthew 5:6 Blessed are they which do hunger and thirst after righteousness: for they shall be filled.

*Matthew 5:10 Blessed are they which are persecuted for righteousness' sake: for theirs is the kingdom of heaven.

*Matthew 5:20 For I say unto you, That except your righteousness shall exceed the righteousness of the scribes and Pharisees, ye shall in no case enter into the kingdom of heaven.

*Matthew 6:33 But seek ye first the kingdom of God, and his righteousness; and all these things shall be added unto you.

*1 Corinthians 15:34 Awake to righteousness, and sin not; for some have not the knowledge of God: I speak this to your shame.

*1 Corinthians 1:30 But of him are ye in Christ Jesus, who of God is made unto us wisdom, and righteousness, and sanctification, and redemption:

---

*Luke 1:75 In holiness and righteousness before him, all the days of our life.

---

*Acts 10:35 But in every nation he that feareth him, and worketh righteousness, is accepted with him.

---

*2 Corinthians 5:21 For he hath made him to be sin for us, who knew no sin; that we might be made the righteousness of God in him.

---

*2 Corinthians 6:7 By the word of truth, by the power of God, by the armour of righteousness on the right hand and on the left,

---

*Romans 6:13 Neither yield ye your members as instruments of unrighteousness unto sin: but yield yourselves unto God, as those that are alive from the dead, and your members as instruments of righteousness unto God.

---

*Romans 6:16 Know ye not, that to whom ye yield yourselves servants to obey, his servants ye are to whom ye obey; whether of sin unto death, or of obedience unto righteousness?

---

*Romans 6:18 Being then made free from sin, ye became the servants of righteousness.

---

*Romans 8:4 That the righteousness of the law might be fulfilled in us, who walk not after the flesh, but after the Spirit.

---

*Titus 2:12 Teaching us that, denying ungodliness and worldly lusts, we should live soberly, righteously, and godly, in this present world;

---

*Romans 14:17 For the kingdom of God is not meat and drink; but righteousness, and peace, and joy in the Holy Ghost.

---

*Ephesians 4:24 And that ye put on the new man, which after God is created in righteousness and true holiness.

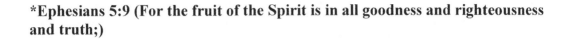

*Ephesians 5:9 (For the fruit of the Spirit is in all goodness and righteousness and truth;)

*1 Timothy 6:11 But thou, O man of God, flee these things; and follow after righteousness, godliness, faith, love, patience, meekness.

*2 Timothy 2:22 Flee also youthful lusts: but follow righteousness, faith, charity, peace, with them that call on the Lord out of a pure heart.

*2 Timothy 3:16 All scripture is given by inspiration of God, and is profitable for doctrine, for reproof, for correction, for instruction in righteousness:

*1 Peter 2:24 Who his own self bare our sins in his own body on the tree, that we, being dead to sins, should live unto righteousness: by whose stripes ye were healed.

*1 John 2:29 If ye know that he is righteous, ye know that every one that doeth righteousness is born of him.

*1 John 3:10 In this the children of God are manifest, and the children of the devil: whosoever doeth not righteousness is not of God, neither he that loveth not his brother.

Shoes of the Gospel of Peace

The third piece of God's armor is represented by the Roman soldier's **Shoe's**! In The days of the Apostle Paul the soldier's feet were outfitted with sandals made up of a thick leather sole and various straps that wrapped up to his ankles. The shoes of Roman soldiers were usually impregnated with bits of metal or nails to give him greater traction as he climbed a slippery hill, and greater stability as he fought. The shoes served a very important purpose: to keep the soldier well planted while marching or standing in unstable soil.

Paul instructed that we as believers outfit our feet with shoes of peace (Eph. 6:15). Like the historical shoes, our spiritual **"shoes of peace"** provide us with the ability to face rough or unknown situations knowing that we won't slip from our positions. It's important to understand that peace is not the absence of tough times. Instead, "You will have many trials, test, and sorrows," Jesus assured (John 16:33). We are not guaranteed smooth and easy paths to walk upon. David revealed this in Psalms 23:

*Psalm 23:4 Yea, though I walk through the valley of the shadow of death, I will fear no evil: for thou art with me; thy rod and thy staff they comfort me.

Even though we are traveling through harsh and dangerous territory, we can still experience peace that passes all understanding. *"I have told you all this so that you may have peace in Me,"* Jesus revealed. **"Peace in Me"** is the most important part of what He said. In this world, peace isn't found in our circumstances, but rather found in Christ. In Christ we have the refreshment and protection of His presence, which is peace. In Christ we also have peace with God, made possible by the work of Christ on the cross.

Since the average ancient soldier marched on rough land, hot roads, climbed over jagged rocks, trampled over thorns, and waded through streambeds of jagged stones, his feet needed much protection. A soldier whose feet were blistered, cut, or swollen could not fight well and often was not able to stand up in the battle. A Christian's spiritual footwear is equally important in his warfare against the schemes of the devil. If he has carefully girded his loins with truth and put on the breastplate of righteousness, but does not properly shod his feet with the "preparation of the gospel of peace" (Ephesians 6:15), he is destined to stumble, fall, and suffer many defeats. If the feet or legs of the foot soldier is materially wounded, a man can not stand to resist his enemy, or pursue him if the enemy flees, nor flee from him should he have the worst of the fight.

*Hebrews 12:15 Looking diligently lest any man fail of the grace of God; lest any root of bitterness springing up trouble you, and thereby many be defiled;

The Greek word translated "preparation" refers to readiness. A good pair of boots allowed the soldier to march, climb, fight, or do whatever else was necessary at a moment's notice. Christ demands the same readiness of His people.The Israelites were commanded to eat the *passover with their feet shod, to show that they were ready for their journey*. And our Lord commands his disciples to be shod with sandals, that they might be ready to go and publish the Gospel, as the Israelites were to go to possess the promised land. Every Christian should consider himself on his journey from a strange land to his own country, and not only stand every moment prepared to proceed, but be every moment in actual progress towards his home.

The believer who stands in the Lord's power need not fear any enemy--even Satan himself. When devils comes to attack us, our feet are rooted firmly on the solid ground of the gospel of peace, through which God provided by the death, and resurrection of Jesus Christ! The gospel of peace is the marvelous truth that in Christ we are now at peace with God and are one with Him. Therefore, when our feet are shod with the preparation of the gospel of peace, we stand in the confidence of God's love for us, His union with us, and His commitment to fight for us. He leads us and guides us with His amazing peace!

The unsaved person is helpless, ungodly, sinful, and an enemy of God (Romans5:6-10).The saved person, on the other hand, is reconciled to God through faith in His Son(Romans 5:10-11; 2 Corinthians 5:20-21).Christ sacrifice brings about peace between God and man, and men with men in society, countries, nations, nationalities, and all the different races! Contentions, strife, quarrels, and all wars, being as alien from its nature and design, as they are opposed to the nature of God is pure and holy love.

*Romans 10:15 And how shall they preach, except they be sent? as it is written, How beautiful are the feet of them that preach the gospel of peace, and bring glad tidings of good things!

*Romans 16:20 And the God of peace shall bruise Satan under your feet shortly. The grace of our Lord Jesus Christ be with you. Amen.

*1 Corinthians 15:25 For he must reign, till he hath put all enemies under his feet.

*Luke 10:19 Behold, I give unto you power to tread on serpents and scorpions, and over all the power of the enemy: and nothing shall by any means hurt you.

*1 Corinthians 15:27 For he hath put all things under his feet. But when he saith all things are put under him, it is manifest that he is excepted, which did put all things under him.

*Ephesians 1:22 And hath put all things under his feet, and gave him to be the head over all things to the church,

*Hebrews 2:8 Thou hast put all things in subjection under his feet. For in that he put all in subjection under him, he left nothing that is not put under him. But now we see not yet all things put under him.

---

*Hebrews 12:13 And make straight paths for your feet, lest that which is lame be turned out of the way; but let it rather be healed.

---

*Psalm 8:6 Thou madest him to have dominion over the works of thy hands; thou hast put all things under his feet:

---

*Psalm 18:33 He maketh my feet like hinds' feet, and setteth me upon my high places.

---

*Psalm 18:36 Thou hast enlarged my steps under me, that my feet did not slip.

---

*Psalm 47:3 He shall subdue the people under us, and the nations under our feet.

---

*Psalm 91:13 Thou shalt tread upon the lion and adder: the young lion and the dragon shalt thou trample under feet.

---

*Psalm 119:101 I have refrained my feet from every evil way, that I might keep thy word.

---

*Psalm 119:105 Thy word is a lamp unto my feet, and a light unto my path.

---

*Philippians 4:7 And the peace of God, which passeth all understanding, shall keep your hearts and minds through Christ Jesus.

---

*John 14:27 Peace I leave with you, my peace I give unto you: not as the world giveth, give I unto you. Let not your heart be troubled, neither let it be afraid.

---

*Colossians 3:15 And let the peace of God rule in your hearts, to the which also ye are called in one body; and be ye thankful.

---

*Isaiah 26:3 Thou wilt keep him in perfect peace, whose mind is stayed on thee: because he trusteth in thee.

*2 Thessalonians 3:16 Now the Lord of peace himself give you peace always by all means. The Lord be with you all.

*Romans 8:6 For to be carnally minded is death; but to be spiritually minded is life and peace.

*Isaiah 48:18 O that thou hadst hearkened to my commandments! then had thy peace been as a river, and thy righteousness as the waves of the sea:

*Isaiah 48:22 There is no peace, saith the Lord, unto the wicked.

*Psalm 29:11 The Lord will give strength unto his people; the Lord will bless his people with peace.

*Galatians 3:28 There is neither Jew nor Greek, there is neither bond nor free, there is neither male nor female: for ye are all one in Christ Jesus.

*Ephesians 2:14 For he is our peace, who hath made both one, and hath broken down the middle wall of partition between us;

The Shield Of Faith

*Ephesians 6:16 Above all, taking the shield of faith, wherewith ye shall be able to quench all the fiery darts of the wicked.

   Above all, (over all the rest of the armor), taking the **shield of faith**. The fourth piece of God's armor is represented by the Roman soldier's **Shield**! Roman soldiers used several kinds of shields. The kind Paul refers to here (Gk., thureos) was about two-and-a-half feet wide and high, designed to protect the entire body of the soldier. The shield was made of a solid piece of wood and was covered with metal or thick leather. In New Testament times the tips of arrows would often be wrapped in pieces of cloth that had been soaked in pitch. Just before the arrow was shot, the tip would be lighted and the flaming missile would be shot at the enemy troops. The pitch burned fiercely, and on impact it would splatter flaming bits, igniting anything flammable in its path. In addition to piercing a person's body, such arrows inflicted serious burns on enemy soldiers and destroyed their clothing and gear. The most reliable protection against these flaming missiles was the Soldiers Shield. Its covering of metal or treated leather would either deflect or extinguish them.

Demonic powers continually bombards God's children with the flaming arrows of immorality, hatred, anger, covetousness, pride, doubt, fear, despair, distrust, and many other temptations. Every temptation, either directly or indirectly, tries to get us to doubt or distrust God. The purpose of Satan's missiles is to cause believers to forsake their trust in God, to drive a wedge between the Savior and the saved. Put up the shield of faith and that won't happen to you. Faith is the grace by which all others are preserved and rendered active, so it is properly represented here under the notion of a shield, by which the whole body is covered and protected.

Faith (Trust, Believe) in **Christ** is the key to our victory! With this truth and reality in our heart, it is expedient that we become full of faith. As we connect the dots from Genesis to Revelation, it becomes quite clear that the cause of all of man's sorrows, shortcomings, immoralities, sicknesses, troubles are due to the fact that we are not truly trusting, looking, depending, relying and having faith in **Christ**! Based upon this fact we must do everything we can to attain more faith. Even the disciples as they watched the life of **Jesus** before their eyes, asked Him to help increase their faith. This is the whole purpose of this book. To provide biblical means by which we can have an increase of faith in **Christ** which causes us to overcome! Please open your heart, your mind, and your life to these realities. And let **Jesus Christ** become your all!

A Brief Description of Faith: It is when God, His Word, His will is Supernaturally Quickened to you by the Holy Spirit! These realities become more real to you than anything in life. It is a revelation of Who Jesus Christ really is & what He has done and is doing. It is a quickening in your heart when you know, that you know, that you know, that you know God is with you, then who can be against you? That Christ Jesus Himself, lives inside of you. Your mind, your will, your emotions, and every part of your being is overwhelmed with the reality of Jesus Christ! And you enter into the realm where all things are possible!

*Proverbs 3:Trust in the Lord with all thine heart; and lean not unto thine own understanding. In all thy ways acknowledge him, and he shall direct thy paths.

---

*2 Corinthians 5:7 - (For we walk by faith, not by sight:)

*Hebrews 11:6 - But without faith [it is] impossible to please [him]: for he that cometh to God must believe that he is, and [that] he is a rewarder of them that diligently seek him.

*1 John 5:4 - For whatsoever is born of God overcometh the world: and this is the victory that overcometh the world, [even] our faith.

*Mark 9:23 - Jesus said unto him, If thou canst believe, all things [are] possible to him that believeth.

*Hebrews 11:1-39 - Now faith is the substance of things hoped for, the evidence of things not seen.

*Hebrews 11:1 - Now faith is the substance of things hoped for, the evidence of things not seen.

*Psalms 40:4 - Blessed [is] that man that maketh the LORD his trust, and respecteth not the proud, nor such as turn aside to lies.

*Mark 11:23 - For verily I say unto you, That whosoever shall say unto this mountain, Be thou removed, and be thou cast into the sea; and shall not doubt in his heart, but shall believe that those things which he saith shall come to pass; he shall have whatsoever he saith.

*John 3:36 - He that believeth on the Son hath everlasting life: and he that believeth not the Son shall not see life; but the wrath of God abideth on him.

*Acts 26:18 - To open their eyes, [and] to turn [them] from darkness to light, and [from] the power of Satan unto God, that they may receive forgiveness of sins, and inheritance among them which are sanctified by faith that is in me.

*James 1:12 - Blessed [is] the man that endureth temptation: for when he is tried, he shall receive the crown of life, which the Lord hath promised to them that love him.

*1 Peter 1:7 - That the trial of your faith, being much more precious than of gold that perisheth, though it be tried with fire, might be found unto praise and honour and glory at the appearing of Jesus Christ:

*1 Corinthians 2:5 - That your faith should not stand in the wisdom of men, but in the power of God.

*Isaiah 40:31 - But they that wait upon the LORD shall renew [their] strength; they shall mount up with wings as eagles; they shall run, and not be weary; [and] they shall walk, and not faint.

*Ephesians 6:10-18 - Finally, my brethren, be strong in the Lord, and in the power of his might.   (Read More...)

*Colossians 2:7 - Rooted and built up in him, and stablished in the faith, as ye have been taught, abounding therein with thanksgiving.

*1 Samuel 17:37 - David said moreover, The LORD that delivered me out of the paw of the lion, and out of the paw of the bear, he will deliver me out of the hand of this Philistine. And Saul said unto David, Go, and the LORD be with thee.

*Revelation 3:20 - Behold, I stand at the door, and knock: if any man hear my voice, and open the door, I will come in to him, and will sup with him, and he with me.

*Hebrews 10:39 - But we are not of them who draw back unto perdition; but of them that believe to the saving of the soul.

*Romans 8:37 - Nay, in all these things we are more than conquerors through him that loved us.

*James 1:6 - But let him ask in faith, nothing wavering. For he that wavereth is like a wave of the sea driven with the wind and tossed.

*Hebrews 11:7 - By faith Noah, being warned of God of things not seen as yet, moved with fear, prepared an ark to the saving of his house; by the which he condemned the world, and became heir of the righteousness which is by faith.

---

*2 Timothy 4:7 - I have fought a good fight, I have finished [my] course, I have kept the faith:

---

*Mark 16:16 - He that believeth and is baptized shall be saved; but he that believeth not shall be damned.

---

*Hebrews 12:2 - Looking unto Jesus the author and finisher of [our] faith; who for the joy that was set before him endured the cross, despising the shame, and is set down at the right hand of the throne of God.

---

*1 Timothy 3:9 - Holding the mystery of the faith in a pure conscience.

---

*Colossians 1:23 - If ye continue in the faith grounded and settled, and [be] not moved away from the hope of the gospel, which ye have heard, [and] which was preached to every creature which is under heaven; whereof I Paul am made a minister;

---

*Romans 10:17 - So then faith [cometh] by hearing, and hearing by the word of God.

---

*1 Peter 1:8 - Whom having not seen, ye love; in whom, though now ye see [him] not, yet believing, ye rejoice with joy unspeakable and full of glory:

*John 6:35 - And Jesus said unto them, I am the bread of life: he that cometh to me shall never hunger; and he that believeth on me shall never thirst.

---

*Colossians 2:7 - Rooted and built up in him, and stablished in the faith, as ye have been taught, abounding therein with thanksgiving.

---

*Romans 10:9 - That if thou shalt confess with thy mouth the Lord Jesus, and shalt believe in thine heart that God hath raised him from the dead, thou shalt be saved.

---

*Psalms 40:4 - Blessed [is] that man that maketh the LORD his trust, and respecteth not the proud, nor such as turn aside to lies.

*Psalms 31:14-15 - But I trusted in thee, O LORD: I said, Thou [art] my God.

*Galatians 5:1 - Stand fast therefore in the liberty wherewith Christ hath made us free, and be not entangled again with the yoke of bondage.

*Isaiah 40:31 - But they that wait upon the LORD shall renew [their] strength; they shall mount up with wings as eagles; they shall run, and not be weary; [and] they shall walk, and not faint.

*Isaiah 26:3-4 - Thou wilt keep [him] in perfect peace, [whose] mind [is] stayed [on thee]: because he trusteth in thee.

*Psalms 37:5-6 - Commit thy way unto the LORD; trust also in him; and he shall bring [it] to pass.

*Mark 11:24 - Therefore I say unto you, What things soever ye desire, when ye pray, believe that ye receive [them], and ye shall have [them].

*Psalm 57:1 Be merciful unto me, O God, be merciful unto me: for my soul trusteth in thee: yea, in the shadow of thy wings will I make my refuge, until these calamities be overpast.

*1 Timothy 6:12 Fight the good fight of faith, lay hold on eternal life, whereunto thou art also called, and hast professed a good profession before many witnesses.

CHAPTER FOUR

The Helmet of Salvation

The fifth piece of God's armor is represented by the Roman soldier's **Helmet,** (Ephesians 6:17), without which a soldier would never enter battle. Some of the helmets were made of thick leather covered with metal plates, and others were of heavy molded or beaten metal. They usually had cheek pieces to protect the face, and nose guard's.

The purpose of the helmet was to protect the **HEAD** from injury, particularly from the dangerous broadsword commonly used in the warfare of that day. The sword was a large, two-handed, double-edged sword that measured three to four feet in length. It was often carried by cavalrymen, who would swing at the heads of enemy soldiers to split their skulls or decapitate them. Head wounds in ancient times were the most common and fatal wounds of war, and no soldier would dare enter battle without this helmet.

When Paul relates the helmet to salvation it indicates that Satan's attacks are directed at the believer's knowledge in Christ. This is a major attack against our mind, our thoughts, and our emotions. Since Paul is addressing believers, putting on the helmet of salvation is not referring to receiving Christ as Savior, but to protecting our minds until our task on earth is completed! It is obvious by Pauls words that the only ones who can take up any piece of God's armor are those who are already born again.

Spiritually speaking, our heads represent what's in them—our minds. We know that the mind is the devil's playground. Satan barges into our lives with thoughts as to why God will not use us, why we'll never be healed, or why our particular sins are too big to be forgiven, or overcome. We may not be able to stop everything that creeps into our minds, but we can take these thoughts captive by the Word of God. (see 2 Cor. 10:4–5). When Satan whispers, "God doesn't love you," take it captive with God's Word: "For God so loved the world that he gave his only Son" (John 3:16). If he accuses, "You've messed up too many times," remind him of the Scripture, "confess your sins, and He is faithful and just to forgive them"

There are given to us amazing promises of conquering every adversary and overcoming every difficulty, through the blood of the Lamb, and the Word of

God. These promises are as a helmet that protects our head; an impenetrable helmet, that the blow of the battle-axe, or broad sword cannot cleave. The hope of continual safety and protection, built on the promises of God, to which the upright follower of Christ has a Divine right, protects the understanding from being darkened, and our judgment from being confused by any temptations of Satan, or subtle arguments of the ungodly. He who carries Christ in his heart, with a renewed mind, cannot be cheated out of eternal life!

*1 Thessalonians 5:8 But let us, who are of the day, be sober, putting on the breastplate of faith and love; and for an helmet, the hope of salvation.

---

*Isaiah 59:17 For he put on righteousness as a breastplate, and an helmet of salvation upon his head; and he put on the garments of vengeance for clothing, and was clad with zeal as a cloak.

---

*Jeremiah 46:3 Order ye the buckler and shield, and draw near to battle.4 Harness the horses; and get up, ye horsemen, and stand forth with your helmets; furbish the spears, and put on the brigandines.

---

*Romans 12:2 And be not conformed to this world: but be ye transformed by the renewing of your mind, that ye may prove what is that good, and acceptable, and perfect, will of God.

---

*Colossians 3:10 And have put on the new man, which is renewed in knowledge after the image of him that created him:

---

*Ephesians 4:22 That ye put off concerning the former conversation the old man, which is corrupt according to the deceitful lusts;23 And be renewed in the spirit of your mind;24 And that ye put on the new man, which after God is created in righteousness and true holiness.

---

*Ephesians 5:17 Wherefore be ye not unwise, but understanding what the will of the Lord is.

---

*Psalm 51:10 Create in me a clean heart, O God; and renew a right spirit within me.

---

*Psalm 19:7 The law of the Lord is perfect, converting the soul: the testimony of the Lord is sure, making wise the simple.

*Colossians 1:21 And you, that were sometime alienated and enemies in your mind by wicked works, yet now hath he reconciled. 22 In the body of his flesh through death, to present you holy and unblameable and unreproveable in his sight:

*Proverbs 23:7 For as he thinketh in his heart, so is he:

*Philippians 4:8 Finally, brethren, whatsoever things are true, whatsoever things are honest, whatsoever things are just, whatsoever things are pure, whatsoever things are lovely, whatsoever things are of good report; if there be any virtue, and if there be any praise, think on these things.

*1 Corinthians 10:12 Wherefore let him that thinketh he standeth take heed lest he fall.

*Galatians 6:3 For if a man think himself to be something, when he is nothing, he deceiveth himself.

*1 Peter 4:12 Beloved, think it not strange concerning the fiery trial which is to try you, as though some strange thing happened unto you:

*2 Corinthians 10:3 For though we walk in the flesh, we do not war after the flesh:
4 (For the weapons of our warfare are not carnal, but mighty through God to the pulling down of strong holds;)5 Casting down imaginations, and every high thing that exalteth itself against the knowledge of God, and bringing into captivity every thought to the obedience of Christ.

*Matthew 10:19 But when they deliver you up, take no thought how or what ye shall speak: for it shall be given you in that same hour what ye shall speak.

1 Corinthians 13:11 When I was a child, I spake as a child, I understood as a child, I thought as a child: but when I became a man, I put away childish things.

Philippians 2:6 Who, being in the form of God, thought it not robbery to be equal with God:

The sword of the Spirit

The sixth piece of God's armor is represented by the Roman soldier's **Sword**. Now you can have the best sword that money could buy, or men could ever make, and yet if you are not proficient in the swords use, your enemy will be able to easily kill and destroy you. A good soldier must consistently be working on his swordsmanship, exercising, and being proficient in its use. Using the sword and shield is not something that just comes naturally, or automatically. We must be taught and trained in their proper use.

*Ephesians 6:17 And take the helmet of salvation, and the sword of the Spirit, which is the word of God:

The sword of which St. Paul speaks is, as he explains it, is the word of God; that is the divine revelation which God has given of himself, and his perfect will for the human race, to the world! It is what we call the Holy Scriptures, the Bible, which has been given to us by the Holy Ghost!

*2 Peter 1:21 For the prophecy came not in old time by the will of man: but holy men of God spake as they were moved by the Holy Ghost.

We can never over emphasize the importance of speaking God's word to the circumstances of life. The word that we speak must be spirit, and it must be quickened by the spirit of life in Christ Jesus. This must be the word of God, that has been hidden in our heart, that is spoken out of our mouth over every situation that is contrary to God's known will.

*2 Corinthians 4:13 We having the same spirit of faith, according as it is written, I believed, and therefore have I spoken; we also believe, and therefore speak;

This is called the sword of the Spirit, because it comes from the Holy Spirit, and receives its fulfillment in the heart of man, spoken from his mouth by the operation of the Holy Spirit. An ability to speak the word of God in times of trials, temptation, afflictions, and attacks of the enemy. With the sword of the spirit, the spoken word of God from our hearts, we can have absolute confidence in defeating the enemy, and every problem that comes against us. The shield of faith, and the sword of the spirit - the word of God, or faith in God's unchangeable word, are the principal armor of the of the soldier of Christ. He in whom the word of God dwells richly, and who has that faith by which he knows that he has redemption, even the forgiveness of sins, need not fear the power of the devil. He stands fast in the liberty wherewith Christ hath made him free.

*Hebrews 4:12 For the word of God is quick, and powerful, and sharper than any two edged sword, piercing even to the dividing asunder of soul and spirit, and of the joints and marrow, and is a discerner of the thoughts and intents of the heart.

*Jeremiah 23:29 Is not my word like as a fire? saith the Lord; and like a hammer that breaketh the rock in pieces?

*Isaiah 55:11 So shall my word be that goeth forth out of my mouth: it shall not return unto me void, but it shall accomplish that which I please, and it shall prosper in the thing whereto I sent it.

*Isaiah 49:2 And he hath made my mouth like a sharp sword; in the shadow of his hand hath he hid me, and made me a polished shaft; in his quiver hath he hid me;

*Revelation 1:16 And he had in his right hand seven stars: and out of his mouth went a sharp two edged sword: and his countenance was as the sun shineth in his strength.

*Revelation 19:15 And out of his mouth goeth a sharp sword, that with it he should smite the nations: and he shall rule them with a rod of iron: and he treadeth the winepress of the fierceness and wrath of Almighty God.

*Mark 11:23 For verily I say unto you, That whosoever shall say unto this mountain, Be thou removed, and be thou cast into the sea; and shall not doubt in his heart, but shall believe that those things which he saith shall come to pass; he shall have whatsoever he saith.

*Matthew 17:20 And Jesus said unto them, Because of your unbelief: for verily I say unto you, If ye have faith as a grain of mustard seed, ye shall say unto this mountain, Remove hence to yonder place; and it shall remove; and nothing shall be impossible unto you.

*Matthew 8:8 The centurion answered and said, Lord, I am not worthy that thou shouldest come under my roof: but speak the word only, and my servant shall be healed.

*Isaiah 46:10 Declaring the end from the beginning, and from ancient times the things that are not yet done, saying, My counsel shall stand, and I will do all my pleasure:

*Jeremiah 5:14 Wherefore thus saith the Lord God of hosts, Because ye speak this word, behold, I will make my words in thy mouth fire, and this people wood, and it shall devour them.

*2 Thessalonians 2:8 And then shall that Wicked be revealed, whom the Lord shall consume with the spirit of his mouth, and shall destroy with the brightness of his coming:

*Romans 10:8 But what saith it? The word is nigh thee, even in thy mouth, and in thy heart: that is, the word of faith, which we preach;9That if thou shalt confess with thy mouth the Lord Jesus, and shalt believe in thine heart that God hath raised him from the dead, thou shalt be saved. 10 For with the heart man believeth unto righteousness; and with the mouth confession is made unto salvation.

*Ephesians 4:29 Let no corrupt communication proceed out of your mouth, but that which is good to the use of edifying, that it may minister grace unto the hearers.

*Revelation 2:16 Repent; or else I will come unto thee quickly, and will fight against them with the sword of my mouth.

*Matthew 4:4 But he answered and said, It is written, Man shall not live by bread alone, but by every word that proceedeth out of the mouth of God.

*Matthew 4:6 And saith unto him, If thou be the Son of God, cast thyself down: for it is written, He shall give his angels charge concerning thee: and in their hands they shall bear thee up, lest at any time thou dash thy foot against a stone.

Praying Always with All Prayer

The seventh piece of God's armor **is Continual Prayer!** The absolute necessity of prayer that he may successfully resist principalities, powers, the rulers of the darkness of this world, and the spiritual wickedness's in heavenly places, with whom we have to contend. The whole armor of God, consists in, **#1** the girdle; **#2** the breast-plate; **#3** the greaves; **#4** the shield; **#5** the helmet; **#6** the sword, **#7** and prayer! He who had these in his armor is completely armed.

Paul the apostle shows that these spiritual warriors must depend on the Captain of their salvation, and pray with all prayer, i.e. incessantly, being always in the spirit of prayer, always depending on Him who can alone save, and who alone can destroy.

*John 15:5 I am the vine, ye are the branches: He that abideth in me, and I in him, the same bringeth forth much fruit: for without me ye can do nothing.

When the apostle exhorts Christians to pray with all prayer, we may at once see that he is speaking about a faith filled, heart felt, fervent, compassionate intimacy with God!

With all prayer - Refers to the different kinds of prayer that is revealed to us in the Word of God! All of these are necessary to the real Christian; the one whose heart is right with God.

1. The Prayer of Agreement
2. The Prayer of Faith
3. The Prayer of Consecration and Dedication
4. The Prayer of Praise and Worship
5. The Prayer of Intercession
6. The Prayer of Binding and Loosing
7. The Prayer of Unity
8. The Prayer of Confession, and Repentance
9. The Prayer of Supplication

Watching thereunto - Being always on your guard lest your enemies should surprise you. **Watch**, not only against evil, but also for opportunities to do good, and for opportunities to receive direction from God. Without watchfulness, and prayer all of the spiritual armor will be useless.

With all perseverance - Being always intent on your mission, and never losing sight of your danger, or of your interest. The word implies stretching out the neck, and looking about, in order to discern an enemy at a distance. A soldier on the battle field must always be on his toes, sober, vigilant, awake!

For all saints - For all Christians; Christ said by our love for one another, the world will know that we are the disciples of Jesus!

*Jeremiah 33:3 Call unto me, and I will answer thee, and show thee great and mighty things, which thou knowest not.
*Psalm 86:7 In the day of my trouble I will call upon thee: for thou wilt answer me.

---

*Psalm 91:15 He shall call upon me, and I will answer him: I will be with him in trouble; I will deliver him, and honour him.16 With long life will I satisfy him, and shew him my salvation.

---

*Psalm 118:5 I called upon the Lord in distress: the Lord answered me, and set me in a large place.

---

*Isaiah 58:9 Then shalt thou call, and the Lord shall answer; thou shalt cry, and he shall say, Here I am. If thou take away from the midst of thee the yoke, the putting forth of the finger, and speaking vanity;

---

*Psalm 55:17 Evening, and morning, and at noon, will I pray, and cry aloud: and he shall hear my voice.

---

*Philippians 4:6 Be careful for nothing; but in every thing by prayer and supplication with thanksgiving let your requests be made known unto God.

---

*Colossians 4:2 Continue in prayer, and watch in the same with thanksgiving;

---

*1 Thessalonians 5:17 Pray without ceasing.

---

*John 15:7 - If ye abide in me, and my words abide in you, ye shall ask what ye will, and it shall be done unto you.

*Mark 11:24 - Therefore I say unto you, What things soever ye desire, when ye pray, believe that ye receive [them], and ye shall have [them].

*Matthew 6:7 - But when ye pray, use not vain repetitions, as the heathen [do]: for they think that they shall be heard for their much speaking.

*Luke 11:9 - And I say unto you, Ask, and it shall be given you; seek, and ye shall find; knock, and it shall be opened unto you.

*Romans 8:26 - Likewise the Spirit also helpeth our infirmities: for we know not what we should pray for as we ought: but the Spirit itself maketh intercession for us with groanings which cannot be uttered.

*Matthew 6:6 - But thou, when thou prayest, enter into thy closet, and when thou hast shut thy door, pray to thy Father which is in secret; and thy Father which seeth in secret shall reward thee openly.

*1 Timothy 2:1-4 - I exhort therefore, that, first of all, supplications, prayers, intercessions, [and] giving of thanks, be made for all men;

*Matthew 26:41 - Watch and pray, that ye enter not into temptation: the spirit indeed [is] willing, but the flesh [is] weak.

*James 5:16 - Confess [your] faults one to another, and pray one for another, that ye may be healed. The effectual fervent prayer of a righteous man availeth much.

*Luke 18:1 - And he spake a parable unto them [to this end], that men ought always to pray, and not to faint;

*Psalms 34:17 - [The righteous] cry, and the LORD heareth, and delivereth them out of all their troubles.

*Matthew 6:5-8 - And when thou prayest, thou shalt not be as the hypocrites [are]: for they love to pray standing in the synagogues and in the corners of the streets, that they may be seen of men. Verily I say unto you, They have their reward.

*Matthew 6:9-13 - After this manner therefore pray ye: Our Father which art in heaven, Hallowed be thy name. (Read More...)

*Matthew 6:1-34 - Take heed that ye do not your alms before men, to be seen of them: otherwise ye have no reward of your Father which is in heaven. (Read More...)

*1 John 3:22 - And whatsoever we ask, we receive of him, because we keep his commandments, and do those things that are pleasing in his sight.

*1 John 5:14-15 - And this is the confidence that we have in him, that, if we ask any thing according to his will, he heareth us: (Read More...)

*John 14:13 And whatsoever ye shall ask in my name, that will I do, that the Father may be glorified in the Son.

*1 Timothy 2:5 - For [there is] one God, and one mediator between God and men, the man Christ Jesus;

*1 John 5:14 - And this is the confidence that we have in him, that, if we ask any thing according to his will, he heareth us:

*James 1:5 - If any of you lack wisdom, let him ask of God, that giveth to all [men] liberally, and upbraideth not; and it shall be given him.:6 - But let him ask in faith, nothing wavering. For he that wavereth is like a wave of the sea driven with the wind and tossed.

*1 Timothy 2:8 - I will therefore that men pray every where, lifting up holy hands, without wrath and doubting.

Gods Mighty Men

David had Mighty Men that were part of his conquering army! It speaks about these mighty men in **2 Samuel 23:8-39**. What is most interesting is the fact that David was one of the first mighty men, and from his example and life came these other man who were tremendously influenced by the life of David. David was a man of faith who inspired others to rise up in the name of God, and take their rightful positions. God has called his people to rise up in his mighty name to conquer and prevail against the enemy. There is no room for passiveness in the kingdom of God. I have known many believers who the years who take the part of acting like an opossum. When the enemy comes, they simply lay down and play dead. This is not humility, but stupidity. God has given to us the weapons we need to overcome every work of the enemy. It is time that we rise up as God's mighty men and women, and put the enemy to flight.

*Leviticus 26:8 And five of you shall chase an hundred, and an hundred of you shall put ten thousand to flight: and your enemies shall fall before you by the sword.

*Hebrews 11:34 Quenched the violence of fire, escaped the edge of the sword, out of weakness were made strong, waxed valiant in fight, turned to flight the armies of the aliens.

I was lying in bed back in 2013 when I literally heard the audible voice of God, and he said to me: **the violent take it by force**! For a while now this has been marinating in my soul. Sometimes when God speaks to me it takes time for it to become a reality. It could be four years later or maybe decades as the spirit of God will be at work on my inside. You could say that it is like a woman when she gets pregnant, life is growing inside of her womb. Even so faith begins as a seed, and must grow within us, in our hearts. We have a lot to do with that faith growing, expanding, enlarging and becoming mature.

Please understand everybody has faith, everybody was born with a measure, a proportion of faith. When Jesus shared the parables about the 10 virgins who were asleep, they all woke up when the trumpet sounded! But Jesus said there were five foolish and five wise. The Five that were wise had enough oil to take them to the arrival of their husband to be. I believe that the oil that Jesus was speaking about is the oil of faith; I believe it's faith in God and Jesus Christ.

People who do not have faith in this time period are really going to have it bad. They're going to try to find somebody that has faith, but it will be too late. And then there are those who have faith which has been in hibernation. Faith can be lying dormant inside of you for many years, and then all of a sudden something supernatural happens and it begins to start to come forth like a bear coming out of hibernation!

When the enemy comes in like a flood, if I will trust God, act upon the word, God will raise up a standard against the enemy. I'm amazed at how many believers are such pacifist when it comes to fighting the fight of faith. You have to rise up in the name of Jesus Christ and speak against that circumstance which is contrary to God's will. If the circumstance does not seem to change, you do not let go of having a heart that is thankful and worshipful towards the Lord.

*2 Chronicles 16:9 For the eyes of the Lord run to and fro throughout the whole earth, to shew himself strong in the behalf of them whose heart is perfect toward him. Herein thou hast done foolishly: therefore from henceforth thou shalt have wars.

*1 Peter 2:9-10 - But ye [are] a chosen generation, a royal priesthood, an holy nation, a peculiar people; that ye should shew forth the praises of him who hath called you out of darkness into his marvellous light:

*1 Corinthians 16:13 - Watch ye, stand fast in the faith, quit you like men, be strong.

*Micah 6:8 - He hath shewed thee, O man, what [is] good; and what doth the LORD require of thee, but to do justly, and to love mercy, and to walk humbly with thy God?

*Job 17:9 The righteous also shall hold on his way, and he that hath clean hands shall be stronger and stronger.

*Philippians 4:13 - I can do all things through Christ which strengtheneth me.

*Deuteronomy 31:6 - Be strong and of a good courage, fear not, nor be afraid of them: for the LORD thy God, he [it is] that doth go with thee; he will not fail thee, nor forsake thee.

*Deuteronomy 20:4 - For the LORD your God [is] he that goeth with you, to fight for you against your enemies, to save you.

*Isaiah 41:10 - Fear thou not; for I [am] with thee: be not dismayed; for I [am] thy God: I will strengthen thee; yea, I will help thee; yea, I will uphold thee with the right hand of my righteousness.

*1 Corinthians 10:13 - There hath no temptation taken you but such as is common to man: but God [is] faithful, who will not suffer you to be tempted above that ye are able; but will with the temptation also make a way to escape, that ye may be able to bear [it].

*Matthew 11:28 - Come unto me, all [ye] that labour and are heavy laden, and I will give you rest.

*2 Corinthians 12:9-10 - And he said unto me, My grace is sufficient for thee: for my strength is made perfect in weakness. Most gladly therefore will I rather glory in my infirmities, that the power of Christ may rest upon me. (Read More...)

*Isaiah 40:31 - But they that wait upon the LORD shall renew [their] strength; they shall mount up with wings as eagles; they shall run, and not be weary; [and] they shall walk, and not faint.

*Psalms 31:24 - Be of good courage, and he shall strengthen your heart, all ye that hope in the LORD.

*1 Corinthians 16:13 - Watch ye, stand fast in the faith, quit you like men, be strong.

*James 5:16 - Confess [your] faults one to another, and pray one for another, that ye may be healed. The effectual fervent prayer of a righteous man availeth much.

*Psalm 18:32 It is God that girdeth me with strength, And maketh my way perfect.

*Psalm 46:1 God is our refuge and strength, A very present help in trouble.

---

*Psalm 22:19 But be not thou far from me, O LORD: O my strength, haste thee to help me.

---

*Psalm 28:7-8 The LORD is my strength and my shield; My heart trusted in him, and I am helped: Therefore my heart greatly rejoiceth; And with my song will I praise him. The LORD is their strength, And he is the saving strength of his anointed.

---

*Psalm 118:14 The LORD is my strength and song, And is become my salvation.

---

*Psalm 119:28 My soul melteth for heaviness: Strengthen thou me according unto thy word.

---

*Deuteronomy 20:4 – For the LORD your God [is] he that goeth with you, to fight for you against your enemies, to save you.

---

*1 Chronicles 16:11 Seek the LORD and his strength, Seek his face continually.

---

*Ephesians 6:10 Finally, my brethren, be strong in the Lord, and in the power of his might.

---

*Isaiah 12:2 Behold, God is my salvation; I will trust, and not be afraid: For the LORD JEHOVAH is my strength and my song; He also is become my salvation.

---

*Habakkuk 3:19 The LORD God is my strength, And he will make my feet like hinds' feet, And he will make me to walk upon mine high places. To the chief singer on my stringed instruments.

---

*Mark 12:30 And thou shalt love the Lord thy God with all thy heart, and with all thy soul, and with all thy mind, and with all thy strength: this is the first commandment.

*Psalm 18:34 He teacheth my hands to war, so that a bow of steel is broken by mine arms.

*Revelation 3:21 To him that overcometh will I grant to sit with me in my throne, even as I also overcame, and am set down with my Father in his throne.

*Psalm 18:29 For by thee I have run through a troop; and by my God have I leaped over a wall.

*Colossians 2:15 And having spoiled principalities and powers, he made a shew of them openly, triumphing over them in it.

*Psalm 144:144 Blessed be the Lord my strength which teacheth my hands to war, and my fingers to fight:

*Proverbs 28:1 The wicked flee when no man pursueth: but the righteous are bold as a lion.

*Deuteronomy 28:7 The Lord shall cause thine enemies that rise up against thee to be smitten before thy face: they shall come out against thee one way, and flee before thee seven ways.

*Psalm 46:2 Therefore will not we fear, though the earth be removed, and though the mountains be carried into the midst of the sea;3 Though the waters thereof roar and be troubled, though the mountains shake with the swelling thereof. Selah.

CHAPTER FIVE

In The Name of the LORD

We know that **Jesus Christ** overcame principalities and powers. He defeated the enemy through his sufferings, sacrificial death and resurrection. That God the **Father** has given him a **name that is above every name**, but there is still something that must be done in order to bring about salvations and conversions. That **name** must be lifted up, it must be **preached,** and **declared, proclaimed** to all the world. We must boast, magnify, and exalt his **name**. It takes faith to proclaim **Jesus**, and as you lift up his name it will bring victory to yourself, and to the listeners.

*Mark 16:15 And he said unto them, Go ye into all the world, and preach the gospel to every creature.

It is our responsibility to exalt the name of **Jesus Christ** because he is our Lord and Savior. The world is going to exalt their gods, football, technology, sports, hobbies, vain amusements, all the things that excite them, but what is it that excites us? What is it that we take pleasure and joy in? What is it that makes us want to shout, dance and run? Is it not **Jesus Christ**, the Lamb of God, our king, our Lord and Savior!

*Colossians 3:4 When Christ, who is our life, shall appear, then shall ye also appear with him in glory.

It really is not that complicated, simply speak from your heart the wonderful name of **Jesus Christ. Jesus** said if we are ashamed of him, then he will be ashamed of us.

*Luke 9:26 For whosoever shall be ashamed of me and of my words, of him shall the Son of man be ashamed, when he shall come in his own glory, and in his Father's, and of the holy angels.

Paul the apostle declared boldly that he was not ashamed of the gospel of **Jesus Christ**. As we boast, magnify and exalt **Jesus Christ,** as we speak to the devils, sickness, circumstances in the name of Jesus Christ, we will see, and experience amazing results. We have the wonderful privilege of proclaiming

Jesus Christ to a lost and dying world. He is the only hope! He is the only answer! He is the only solution! Do you believe this?

*Romans 1:16 For I am not ashamed of the gospel of Christ: for it is the power of God unto salvation to everyone that believeth; to the Jew first, and also to the Greek.

Paul declared that he boasted of **Christ** to the Corinthian's, and that he was not ashamed in his boasting. If time would permit, we could look at the attitude of true believers throughout the ages. There are some wonderful and astounding Scriptures in the Old Testament of how the saints of old loved to magnify the name of God. That which we love and believe in is that which we will exalt and boast about. Too many believers are boasting on the devil, his shenanigans and his works without even realizing it. I refuse to boast on the devil and his demonic activities! **I will exalt and magnify the Lord who is worthy to be praised. I will speak the name of Jesus to that which is contrary to the will of God!**

*Matthew 18:20 For where two or three are gathered together in my name, there am I in the midst of them.

*Mark 16:17 And these signs shall follow them that believe; In my name shall they cast out devils; they shall speak with new tongues;18 They shall take up serpents; and if they drink any deadly thing, it shall not hurt them; they shall lay hands on the sick, and they shall recover.

*John 14:13 And whatsoever ye shall ask in my name, that will I do, that the Father may be glorified in the Son.14 If ye shall ask any thing in my name, I will do it.

*John 15:16 Ye have not chosen me, but I have chosen you, and ordained you, that ye should go and bring forth fruit, and that your fruit should remain: that whatsoever ye shall ask of the Father in my name, he may give it you.

*John 16:23 And in that day ye shall ask me nothing. Verily, verily, I say unto you, What so ever ye shall ask the Father in my name, he will give it you. Hitherto have ye asked nothing in my name: ask, and ye shall receive, that your joy may be full.

*Psalm 44:5 Through thee will we push down our enemies: through thy name will we tread them under that rise up against us.

*Psalm 118:10 All nations compassed me about: but in the name of the Lord will I destroy them.11 They compassed me about; yea, they compassed me about: but in the name of the Lord I will destroy them.12 They compassed me about like bees: they are quenched as the fire of thorns: for in the name of the Lord I will destroy them.

*Philippians 2:9 Wherefore God also hath highly exalted him, and given him a name which is above every name:10 That at the name of Jesus every knee should bow, of things in heaven, and things in earth, and things under the earth;11 And that every tongue should confess that Jesus Christ is Lord, to the glory of God the Father.

*Matthew 28:18 And Jesus came and spake unto them, saying, All power is given unto me in heaven and in earth.

*Ephesians 1:19 And what is the exceeding greatness of his power to us-ward who believe, according to the working of his mighty power,20 Which he wrought in Christ, when he raised him from the dead, and set him at his own right hand in the heavenly places,21 Far above all principality, and power, and might, and dominion, and every name that is named, not only in this world, but also in that which is to come:22 And hath put all things under his feet, and gave him to be the head over all things to the church,23 Which is his body, the fulness of him that filleth all in all.

*Mark 9:41 For whosoever shall give you a cup of water to drink in my name, because ye belong to Christ, verily I say unto you, he shall not lose his reward.

It Is Written

When Christ was tempted of the devil (after 40 days of fasting in the wilderness), he came against him with the famous declaration **"It Is Written"**. This powerful statement is used over 80 times throughout the Bible. Based upon the written word of God, Christ overcame the enemy in the wilderness. It only took Jesus declaring: **It Is Written**, three times to cause the enemy to flee. What a wonderful example, illustration Christ gave us in how to defeat the enemy. The brother of Christ (James) gives us wonderful insight when he said:

*James 4:7 Submit yourselves therefore to God. Resist the devil, and he will flee from you.

Submit to God – to obey all of God's directions, and his perfect known will.

Resist the devil - this word resist is a military term that means to stand against. The devil cannot conquer you if you continue to resist, stand against, come against his lies and deceptions. As strong as our enemy is, God never permits him to conquer the man who continues to resist him; he cannot overtake our human will. He who, in the mighty name of Jesus, opposes even the devil himself, is guaranteed to have a speedy and glorious conquest. The devil flees from that name which is above every name, and from the wonderful blood of Jesus Christ.

Every time the enemy comes against us whether by trials, tests, tribulations, temptations, we should boldly declare: **It Is Written**! In order to do this though we must know the word of God. The word of God must be hidden in our heart, and spoken out of our mouth at the appropriate time, in every situation.

*Hebrews 10:7 Then said I, Lo, I come (in the volume of the book it is written of me,) to do thy will, O God.

---

*2 Corinthians 4:13 We having the same spirit of faith, according as it is written, I believed, and therefore have I spoken; we also believe, and therefore speak;

---

*1 Peter 1:16 Because it is written, Be ye holy; for I am holy.

---

*1 John 5:13 These things have I written unto you that believe on the name of the Son of God; that ye may know that ye have eternal life, and that ye may believe on the name of the Son of God.

---

*Revelation 19:16 And he hath on his vesture and on his thigh a name written, King Of Kings, And Lord Of Lords.

---

*Joshua 1:8 This book of the law shall not depart out of thy mouth; but thou shalt meditate therein day and night, that thou mayest observe to do according to all that is written therein: for then thou shalt make thy way prosperous, and then thou shalt have good success.

---

*Joshua 23:6 Be ye therefore very courageous to keep and to do all that is written in the book of the law of Moses, that ye turn not aside therefrom to the right hand or to the left;

*1 Kings 2:3 And keep the charge of the Lord thy God, to walk in his ways, to keep his statutes, and his commandments, and his judgments, and his testimonies, as it is written in the law of Moses, that thou mayest prosper in all that thou doest, and whithersoever thou turnest thyself:

*Psalm 40:7 Then said I, Lo, I come: in the volume of the book it is written of me,

*Matthew 4:4 But he answered and said, It is written, Man shall not live by bread alone, but by every word that proceedeth out of the mouth of God.

*Matthew 4:10 Then saith Jesus unto him, Get thee hence, Satan: for it is written, Thou shalt worship the Lord thy God, and him only shalt thou serve.

*Matthew 21:13 And said unto them, It is written, My house shall be called the house of prayer; but ye have made it a den of thieves.

*Mark 7:6 He answered and said unto them, Well hath Esaias prophesied of you hypocrites, as it is written, This people honoureth me with their lips, but their heart is far from me.

*Luke 4:17 And there was delivered unto him the book of the prophet Esaias. And when he had opened the book, he found the place where it was written, 18 The Spirit of the Lord is upon me, because he hath anointed me to preach the gospel to the poor; he hath sent me to heal the brokenhearted, to preach deliverance to the captives, and recovering of sight to the blind, to set at liberty them that are bruised,

*John 12:13 Took branches of palm trees, and went forth to meet him, and cried, Hosanna: Blessed is the King of Israel that cometh in the name of the Lord.14 And Jesus, when he had found a young ass, sat thereon; as it is written,15 Fear not, daughter of Sion: behold, thy King cometh, sitting on an ass's colt.

*John 20:31 But these are written, that ye might believe that Jesus is the Christ, the Son of God; and that believing ye might have life through his name.

---

*Acts 13:29 And when they had fulfilled all that was written of him, they took him down from the tree, and laid him in a sepulchre.

---

*Romans 1:17 For therein is the righteousness of God revealed from faith to faith: as it is written, The just shall live by faith.

---

*Romans 3:10 As it is written, There is none righteous, no, not one:

---

*Romans 4:17 (As it is written, I have made thee a father of many nations,) before him whom he believed, even God, who quickeneth the dead, and calleth those things which be not as though they were.

---

*Romans 9:33 As it is written, Behold, I lay in Sion a stumblingstone and rock of offence: and whosoever believeth on him shall not be ashamed.

---

*Romans 10:15 And how shall they preach, except they be sent? as it is written, How beautiful are the feet of them that preach the gospel of peace, and bring glad tidings of good things!

---

*Romans 11:26 And so all Israel shall be saved: as it is written, There shall come out of Sion the Deliverer, and shall turn away ungodliness from Jacob:

---

*Romans 14:11 For it is written, As I live, saith the Lord, every knee shall bow to me, and every tongue shall confess to God.

---

*Romans 15:3 For even Christ pleased not himself; but, as it is written, The reproaches of them that reproached thee fell on me.

---

*Romans 15:9 And that the Gentiles might glorify God for his mercy; as it is written, For this cause I will confess to thee among the Gentiles, and sing unto thy name.

---

*1 Corinthians 1:19 For it is written, I will destroy the wisdom of the wise, and will bring to nothing the understanding of the prudent.

*1 Corinthians 1:31 That, according as it is written, He that glorieth, let him glory in the Lord.

*1 Corinthians 2:9 But as it is written, Eye hath not seen, nor ear heard, neither have entered into the heart of man, the things which God hath prepared for them that love him.

*1 Corinthians 9:9 For it is written in the law of Moses, thou shalt not muzzle the mouth of the ox that treadeth out the corn. Doth God take care for oxen?

*1 Corinthians 10:11 Now all these things happened unto them for examples: and they are written for our admonition, upon whom the ends of the world are come.

*1 Corinthians 15:45 And so it is written, The first man Adam was made a living soul; the last Adam was made a quickening spirit.

*Revelation 20:15 And whosoever was not found written in the book of life was cast into the lake of fire.

The Divine Nature

*2 Peter 1:3 According as his divine power hath given unto us all things that pertain unto life and godliness, through the knowledge of him that hath called us to glory and virtue:4 Whereby are given unto us exceeding great and precious promises: that by these ye might be partakers of the <u>divine nature,</u> having escaped the corruption that is in the world through lust.

That by these (Promises) ye might be partakers - The purpose of God's promises was to bring fallen man back to the likeness of God, which he had lost. This, indeed, is the complete purpose of the redemptive work of Christ. We have partaken of an earthly, sensual, and devilish nature; and now the design of God by Christ is to remove this fleshly nature, and to make us partakers of the Divine nature. Christ came to save us from the corruption of ungodly, and impure desiree; desires to have, to do, and to be, that which is against the nature of God himself.

This lustful demonic nature is to be rooted out; and to be replaced by the love which is of God, towards God and man. God has promised to purify our hearts by faith; by the washing of the water of the word. This blessing may be experienced by those who are continually escaping, fleeing from the corruption that is in the world, and in themselves by the apprehension of God's divine promises.

*James 1:21 Wherefore lay apart all filthiness and superfluity of naughtiness, and receive with meekness the engrafted word, which is able to save your souls.

By these amazing truths which the apostle Peter shares with us, we can be possessors of the divine nature of God, which are supernatural weapons which are used against the enemy. By these promises we are sanctified, purified, cleansed, and made whole by Christ. By the spirit, the word, the promises of God we overcome the world, the flesh, and the devil.

*1 John 3:1 Behold, what manner of love the Father hath bestowed upon us, that we should be called the sons of God: therefore the world knoweth us not, because it knew him not.2 Beloved, now are we the sons of God, and it doth not yet appear what we shall be: but we know that, when he shall appear, we shall be like him; for we shall see him as he is.3 And every man that hath this hope in him purifieth himself, even as he is pure.

*John 1:12 But as many as received him, to them gave he power to become the sons of God, even to them that believe on his name:13 Which were born, not of blood, nor of the will of the flesh, nor of the will of man, but of God.

*Romans 8:2 For the law of the Spirit of life in Christ Jesus hath made me free from the law of sin and death.

*2 Corinthians 5:17 Therefore if any man be in Christ, he is a new creature: old things are passed away; behold, all things are become new.

*John 17:17 Sanctify them through thy truth: thy word is truth.

*Luke 8:15 But that on the good ground are they, which in an honest and good heart, having heard the word, keep it, and bring forth fruit with patience.

*James 1:21 Wherefore lay apart all filthiness and superfluity of naughtiness, and receive with meekness the engrafted word, which is able to save your souls.

*Psalm 119:11 Thy word have I hid in mine heart, that I might not sin against thee.

*Psalm 19:7 The law of the Lord is perfect, converting the soul: the testimony of the Lord is sure, making wise the simple.8 The statutes of the Lord are right, rejoicing the heart: the commandment of the Lord is pure, enlightening the eyes.9 The fear of the Lord is clean, enduring forever: the judgments of the Lord are true and righteous altogether.

*2 Corinthians 3:18 But we all, with open face beholding as in a glass the glory of the Lord, are changed into the same image from glory to glory, even as by the Spirit of the Lord.

*Ephesians 5:25 Husbands, love your wives, even as Christ also loved the church, and gave himself for it;26 That he might sanctify and cleanse it with the washing of water by the word,27 That he might present it to himself a glorious church, not having spot, or wrinkle, or any such thing; but that it should be holy and without blemish.

18 Important Characteristics

when we are born again, there is impregnated, imparted within our hearts the seed of the divine nature of Christ. This incorruptible seed of Christ is the divine nature of God at work in us.

*Ephesians 3:20Now unto him that is able to do exceeding abundantly above all that we ask or think, according to the power that worketh in us,

Within this divine nature there is placed within our hearts certain wonderful qualities and attributes that must be developed and matured. These virtues, characteristics, attributes are actually powerful weapons against our enemy, and his demonic hordes. I will list each one of these attributes, and then we will study them. Each one of these wonderful attributes are revealed, strengthened, and developed by the promises of God's word, and acting upon them.

#1 Diligence, #2 Faithfulness, #3 Virtue, #4 Knowledge, #5 Temperance, #6 Patients, #7 Godliness, #8 Brotherly Kindness, #9 Charity, #10 Joy, #11 Goodness, #12 Meekness, #13 Peace, #14 Longsuffering, #15 Gentleness, #16 Holiness, #17 Mercy, #18 Reverence.

*2 Peter 1:5 And beside this, giving all diligence, add to your faith virtue; and to virtue knowledge;6 And to knowledge temperance; and to temperance patience; and to patience godliness;7 And to godliness brotherly kindness; and to brotherly kindness charity.8 For if these things be in you, and abound, they make you that ye shall neither be barren nor unfruitful in the knowledge of our Lord Jesus Christ.9 But he that lacketh these things is blind, and cannot see afar off, and hath forgotten that he was purged from his old sins.10 Wherefore the rather, brethren, give diligence to make your calling and election sure: for if ye do these things, ye shall never fall:

*Galatians 5:22 But the fruit of the Spirit is love, joy, peace, longsuffering, gentleness, goodness, faith, Meekness, temperance: against such there is no law.

Diligence

According to the Oxford Universal Dictionary, diligence is "careful attention, industry, assiduity; unremitting application, persistent endeavor." A diligent person is described as "assiduous, industrious, conscientious, thorough; not idle, not negligent, not lazy." To exert tremendous effort, careful and continued hard work, attentive and persistent effort,

*Proverbs 13:4 - The soul of the sluggard desireth, and [hath] nothing: but the soul of the diligent shall be made fat.

*Proverbs 10:4 - He becometh poor that dealeth [with] a slack hand: but the hand of the diligent maketh rich.

*Galatians 6:9 - And let us not be weary in well doing: for in due season we shall reap, if we faint not.

*1 Corinthians 15:58 - Therefore, my beloved brethren, be ye stedfast, unmoveable, always abounding in the work of the Lord, forasmuch as ye know that your labour is not in vain in the Lord.

*Proverbs 4:23 Keep thy heart with all diligence; for out of it are the issues of life.

*Proverbs 22:29 - Seest thou a man diligent in his business? he shall stand before kings; he shall not stand before mean [men].

*2 Timothy 2:15 - Study to shew thyself approved unto God, a workman that needeth not to be ashamed, rightly dividing the word of truth.

*Proverbs 12:24 - The hand of the diligent shall bear rule: but the slothful shall be under tribute.

*2 Peter 3:14 - Wherefore, beloved, seeing that ye look for such things, be diligent that ye may be found of him in peace, without spot, and blameless.

*2 Peter 1:10 - Wherefore the rather, brethren, give diligence to make your calling and election sure: for if ye do these things, ye shall never fall:

*Ecclesiastes 9:10 - Whatsoever thy hand findeth to do, do [it] with thy might; for [there is] no work, nor device, nor knowledge, nor wisdom, in the grave, whither thou goest.

*Proverbs 11:27 - He that diligently seeketh good procureth favour: but he that seeketh mischief, it shall come unto him.

*James 1:12 - Blessed [is] the man that endureth temptation: for when he is tried, he shall receive the crown of life, which the Lord hath promised to them that love him.

*Proverbs 13:4 The soul of the sluggard desireth, and hath nothing: but the soul of the diligent shall be made fat.

*Philippians 3:14 - I press toward the mark for the prize of the high calling of God in Christ Jesus.

*Psalm 119:4 Thou hast commanded us to keep thy precepts diligently.

*Hebrews 11:6 But without faith it is impossible to please him: for he that cometh to God must believe that he is, and that he is a rewarder of them that diligently seek him.

*Hebrews 12:15 Looking diligently lest any man fail of the grace of God; lest any root of bitterness springing up trouble you, and thereby many be defiled;

Faithfulness

Faithfulness is a characteristics of God's nature. It denotes being faithful, loyal, constant, staunch, steadfast, resolute, firm in adherence to whatever one owes allegiance to. It implies unswerving adherence to a person or thing or to an oath or promise by which you have made a promise.

Proverbs 28:20 - A faithful man shall abound with blessings: but he that maketh haste to be rich shall not be innocent.

Luke 16:10-12 - He that is faithful in that which is least is faithful also in much: and he that is unjust in the least is unjust also in much.

Deuteronomy 28:1-68 - And it shall come to pass, if thou shalt hearken diligently unto the voice of the LORD thy God, to observe [and] to do all his commandments which I command thee this day, that the LORD thy God will set thee on high above all nations of the earth:

Psalm 12:1 Help, Lord; for the godly man ceaseth; for the faithful fail from among the children of men.

Hebrews 13:8 - Jesus Christ the same yesterday, and to day, and for ever.

Psalm 31:23 O love the Lord, all ye his saints: for the Lord preserveth the faithful, and plentifully rewardeth the proud doer.

Psalm 101:6 Mine eyes shall be upon the faithful of the land, that they may dwell with me: he that walketh in a perfect way, he shall serve me.

1 Corinthians 10:13 - There hath no temptation taken you but such as is common to man: but God [is] faithful, who will not suffer you to be tempted above that ye are able; but will with the temptation also make a way to escape, that ye may be able to bear [it].

1 John 1:9 - If we confess our sins, he is faithful and just to forgive us [our] sins, and to cleanse us from all unrighteousness.

Psalms 91:4 - He shall cover thee with his feathers, and under his wings shalt thou trust: his truth [shall be thy] shield and buckler.

1 Corinthians 4:2 - Moreover it is required in stewards, that a man be found faithful.

Psalm 119:90 Thy faithfulness is unto all generations: thou hast established the earth, and it abideth.

1 Thessalonians 5:24 Faithful is he that calleth you, who also will do it.

2 Thessalonians 3:3 But the Lord is faithful, who shall stablish you, and keep you from evil.

2 Timothy 2:11 It is a faithful saying: For if we be dead with him, we shall also live with him:

Hebrews 10:23 Let us hold fast the profession of our faith without wavering; (for he is faithful that promised;)

1 John 1:9 If we confess our sins, he is faithful and just to forgive us our sins, and to cleanse us from all unrighteousness.

Virtue

Courage or fortitude, also moral excellence, moral character, perfection, uprightness, conformity to a standard of right.

*Philippians 4:8 - Finally, brethren, whatsoever things are true, whatsoever things [are] honest, whatsoever things [are] just, whatsoever things [are] pure, whatsoever things [are] lovely, whatsoever things [are] of good report; if [there be] any virtue, and if [there be] any praise, think on these things.

*Proverbs 12:4 A virtuous woman is a crown to her husband: but she that maketh ashamed is as rottenness in his bones.

*Proverbs 31:10 Who can find a virtuous woman? for her price is far above rubies.

*Deuteronomy 31:6 Be strong and of a good courage, fear not, nor be afraid of them: for the Lord thy God, he it is that doth go with thee; he will not fail thee, nor forsake thee.

*Joshua 1:6 Be strong and of a good courage: for unto this people shalt thou divide for an inheritance the land, which I sware unto their fathers to give them.

*Joshua 1:9 Have not I commanded thee? Be strong and of a good courage; be not afraid, neither be thou dismayed: for the Lord thy God is with thee whithersoever thou goest.

*Psalm 27:14 Wait on the Lord: be of good courage, and he shall strengthen thine heart: wait, I say, on the Lord.

*Psalm 31:24 Be of good courage, and he shall strengthen your heart, all ye that hope in the Lord.

*Daniel 11:32 And such as do wickedly against the covenant shall he corrupt by flatteries: but the people that do know their God shall be strong, and do exploits.

---

*Proverbs 14:26 In the fear of the Lord is strong confidence: and his children shall have a place of refuge.

---

*Proverbs 18:10 The name of the Lord is a strong tower: the righteous runneth into it, and is safe.

---

*Ephesians 6:10 Finally, my brethren, be strong in the Lord, and in the power of his might.

---

*Proverbs 28:1 The wicked flee when no man pursueth: but the righteous are bold as a lion.

Knowledge

All knowledge of God or divine truths comes by way of **revelation**. Human knowledge of God is revealed knowledge (revelation) since God, and He alone, can give this knowledge. He bridges the gap between Himself and humanity, disclosing Himself and His will to them. By God alone can God be known. Biblical faith affirms revelation is real because God has chosen to let humans to know Him. The question remains, "How can a person know God." The Bible appears to distinguish two ways of knowing God, general and special revelation.

The Scriptures point to Jesus Christ as God's final revelation to mankind. God has provided ongoing generations of believers a source of knowledge about Himself and His Son. That source is the Bible. Definition of the word revelation: It means an uncovering, removing the veil, a revealing of what was previously unknown. Revelation of God is God's manifestation of Himself to humankind in such a way that men and women can know him, and fellowship with Him. Jesus explained to Peter:

*Matthew 16:17 And Jesus answered and said unto him, Blessed art thou, Simon Barjona: for flesh and blood hath not revealed it unto thee, but my Father which is in heaven.

The knowledge of who Jesus is was not attained by human discovery, nor could it have been; it came from God alone! It is by this knowledge, revelation we overcome the enemy!

*Ephesians 1:17 That the God of our Lord Jesus Christ, the Father of glory, may give unto you the spirit of wisdom and revelation in the knowledge of him:

*2 Corinthians 12:1 It is not expedient for me doubtless to glory. I will come to visions and revelations of the Lord.

*Galatians 1:12 For I neither received it of man, neither was I taught it, but by the revelation of Jesus Christ.

*Ephesians 3:3 How that by revelation he made known unto me the mystery; (as I wrote afore in few words,

*1 Peter 1:13 Wherefore gird up the loins of your mind, be sober, and hope to the end for the grace that is to be brought unto you at the revelation of Jesus Christ;

*Proverbs 18:15 - The heart of the prudent getteth knowledge; and the ear of the wise seeketh knowledge.

*Proverbs 2:10 - When wisdom entereth into thine heart, and knowledge is pleasant unto thy soul;

*Proverbs 1:7 - The fear of the LORD [is] the beginning of knowledge: [but] fools despise wisdom and instruction.

*Hosea 4:6-7 - My people are destroyed for lack of knowledge: because thou hast rejected knowledge, I will also reject thee, that thou shalt be no priest to me: seeing thou hast forgotten the law of thy God, I will also forget thy children.

*Proverbs 8:10 - Receive my instruction, and not silver; and knowledge rather than choice gold.

*Proverbs 24:5 - A wise man [is] strong; yea, a man of knowledge increaseth strength.

*Proverbs 15:14 - The heart of him that hath understanding seeketh knowledge: but the mouth of fools feedeth on foolishness.

*Proverbs 12:1 - Whoso loveth instruction loveth knowledge: but he that hateth reproof [is] brutish.

*Proverbs 3:1-35 - My son, forget not my law; but let thine heart keep my commandments: (Read More...)

*Proverbs 2:1-22 - My son, if thou wilt receive my words, and hide my commandments with thee;   (Read More...)

*Psalms 119:66 - Teach me good judgment and knowledge: for I have believed thy commandments.

*Hosea 4:6 - My people are destroyed for lack of knowledge: because thou hast rejected knowledge, I will also reject thee, that thou shalt be no priest to me: seeing thou hast forgotten the law of thy God, I will also forget thy children.

*1 Corinthians 12:8 - For to one is given by the Spirit the word of wisdom; to another the word of knowledge by the same Spirit;

*Proverbs 1:22 - How long, ye simple ones, will ye love simplicity? and the scorners delight in their scorning, and fools hate knowledge?

CHAPTER SIX

Temperance

Temperance is the proof that Jesus is MY Lord! Many of the problems that Christians get into, are caused by not saying no to their flesh! Discipline is a major aspect of the Christian life. Many broken friendships, and many harsh words come, as a result of not learning how to be temperate. Too many Christians take the attitude that they cannot control their temper, their thoughts, or their actions. This is simply not true. With God's Holy Spirit, and the promises of God we can practice temperance. The meaning of Temperance is being able to master your own desires and passions – to not be controlled by fleshly desires and passions! In the military as soldier we must live in strict discipline – so that we can WIN the war!

*Titus 1:7 For a bishop must be blameless, as the steward of God; not selfwilled, not soon angry, not given to wine, no striker, not given to filthy lucre;8 But a lover of hospitality, a lover of good men, sober, just, holy, temperate;9 Holding fast the faithful word as he hath been taught, that he may be able by sound doctrine both to exhort and to convince the gainsayers.

TEMPERANCE is bringing all of your flesh under the absolute control of Jesus Christ, being Sober, and vigilant. The ability to say:

"No To The World, No to the Flesh, and No to the devil"

Temperance is a Gift from God (2Tim 1:7) Temperance is Something that must be Worked at (2Pet 1:5,6) A good example of Temperance (Dan 1:8-16)

*Acts 24:25 And as he reasoned of righteousness, temperance, and judgment to come, Felix trembled, and answered, Go thy way for this time; when I have a convenient season, I will call for thee.

*1 Corinthians 9:25 And every man that striveth for the mastery is temperate in all things. Now they do it to obtain a corruptible crown; but we an incorruptible.

*1 Corinthians 12:24 For our comely parts have no need: but God hath tempered the body together, having given more abundant honour to that part which lacked.

*Galatians 5:23 Meekness, temperance: against such there is no law.

*Titus 1:8 But a lover of hospitality, a lover of good men, sober, just, holy, temperate;

*Titus 2:2 That the aged men be sober, grave, temperate, sound in faith, in charity, in patience.

*2 Peter 1:6 And to knowledge temperance; and to temperance patience; and to patience godliness;

*1 Corinthians 9:27 - But I keep under my body, and bring [it] into subjection: lest that by any means, when I have preached to others, I myself should be a castaway.

*Galatians 5:22-25 - But the fruit of the Spirit is love, joy, peace, longsuffering, gentleness, goodness, faith,   (Read More...)

*Titus 2:12 - Teaching us that, denying ungodliness and worldly lusts, we should live soberly, righteously, and godly, in this present world;

*2 Peter 1:6 - And to knowledge temperance; and to temperance patience; and to patience godliness;

*Romans 12:1-2 - I beseech you therefore, brethren, by the mercies of God, that ye present your bodies a living sacrifice, holy, acceptable unto God, [which is] your reasonable service.   (Read More...)

*Romans 13:14 - But put ye on the Lord Jesus Christ, and make not provision for the flesh, to [fulfil] the lusts [thereof].

*Proverbs 25:16 - Hast thou found honey? eat so much as is sufficient for thee, lest thou be filled therewith, and vomit it.

---

*1 Peter 5:8 - Be sober, be vigilant; because your adversary the devil, as a roaring lion, walketh about, seeking whom he may devour:

---

*1 Corinthians 9:25 - And every man that striveth for the mastery is temperate in all things. Now they [do it] to obtain a corruptible crown; but we an incorruptible.

Patience

Patience is a willingness to wait upon God, and his will. As Believers we are called upon to be patient in our walk with God, in our relationship with one another, and the circumstances of life. In the midst of this patience we must bear it without complaining, temper tantrums, irritation, or discouragement. A patience that is quiet, a steady perseverance, with diligence. Having patience means you remain calm, even when it seems like you've been waiting forever. It is the ability to accept or tolerate delay, trouble, or suffering without getting angry, upset, bitter, or discouraged.

*Hebrews 10:36 For ye have need of patience, that, after ye have done the will of God, ye might receive the promise.

---

*Romans 12:12 - Rejoicing in hope; patient in tribulation; continuing instant in prayer;

---

*Romans 8:25 - But if we hope for that we see not, [then] do we with patience wait for [it].

---

*Galatians 6:9 - And let us not be weary in well doing: for in due season we shall reap, if we faint not.

---

*Psalms 37:7-9 - Rest in the LORD, and wait patiently for him: fret not thyself because of him who prospereth in his way, because of the man who bringeth wicked devices to pass.

*Philippians 4:6 - Be careful for nothing; but in everything by prayer and supplication with thanksgiving let your requests be made known unto God.

*Ecclesiastes 7:9 - Be not hasty in thy spirit to be angry: for anger resteth in the bosom of fools.

*Ephesians 4:2 - With all lowliness and meekness, with longsuffering, forbearing one another in love;

*1 Peter 2:19-23 - For this [is] thankworthy, if a man for conscience toward God endure grief, suffering wrongfully.

*Romans 5:4 - And patience, experience; and experience, hope:

*James 1:19 - Wherefore, my beloved brethren, let every man be swift to hear, slow to speak, slow to wrath:

*Proverbs 15:18 - A wrathful man stirreth up strife: but [he that is] slow to anger appeaseth strife.

*Isaiah 40:31 - But they that wait upon the LORD shall renew [their] strength; they shall mount up with wings as eagles; they shall run, and not be weary; [and] they shall walk, and not faint.

*Romans 15:5 Now the God of patience and consolation grant you to be likeminded one toward another according to Christ Jesus.

*Colossians 1:11 Strengthened with all might, according to his glorious power, unto all patience and longsuffering with joyfulness;

*1 Timothy 6:11 But thou, O man of God, flee these things; and follow after righteousness, godliness, faith, love, patience, meekness.

*Hebrews 6:12 That ye be not slothful, but followers of them who through faith and patience inherit the promises.

*James 1:3 Knowing this, that the trying of your faith worketh patience. 4 But let patience have her perfect work, that ye may be perfect and entire, wanting nothing.

*James 5:11 Behold, we count them happy which endure. Ye have heard of the patience of Job, and have seen the end of the Lord; that the Lord is very pitiful, and of tender mercy.

*Revelation 2:3 And hast borne, and hast patience, and for my name's sake hast laboured, and hast not fainted.

*Revelation 2:19 I know thy works, and charity, and service, and faith, and thy patience, and thy works; and the last to be more than the first.

Godliness

GOD'LINESS, comes from the word godly = Piety; belief in God, and reverence for his character, his nature, and his laws. It is a careful observance of the laws of God, the keeping of religious duties, proceeding from our love and reverence for the divine character and commandments of God. To be God-like, Pious; reverencing God, and his character and laws. Living in obedience to God's commands, from a principle of love to him and reverence of his character and precepts; religious; righteous; as a godly person. To be conformed to God's law; as a godly life. Piety towards God; a deep, reverential, religious fear; not only worshipping God with outward evidence, but adoring, loving, and magnifying him in the heart.

*2 Timothy 3:5 Having a form of godliness, but denying the power thereof: from such turn away.

*1 Timothy 2:2 For kings, and for all that are in authority; that we may lead a quiet and peaceable life in all godliness and honesty.

*1 Timothy 2:10 But (which becometh women professing godliness) with good works.

*1 Timothy 3:16 And without controversy great is the mystery of godliness: God was manifest in the flesh, justified in the Spirit, seen of angels, preached unto the Gentiles, believed on in the world, received up into glory.

*1 Timothy 4:7 But refuse profane and old wives' fables, and exercise thyself rather unto godliness.

*1 Timothy 4:8 For bodily exercise profiteth little: but godliness is profitable unto all things, having promise of the life that now is, and of that which is to come.

*1 Timothy 6:3 If any man teach otherwise, and consent not to wholesome words, even the words of our Lord Jesus Christ, and to the doctrine which is according to godliness;

*1 Timothy 6:5 Perverse disputings of men of corrupt minds, and destitute of the truth, supposing that gain is godliness: from such withdraw thyself.

*1 Timothy 6:6 But godliness with contentment is great gain.

*1 Timothy 6:11 But thou, O man of God, flee these things; and follow after righteousness, godliness, faith, love, patience, meekness.

*2 Timothy 3:5 Having a form of godliness, but denying the power thereof: from such turn away.

*Titus 1:1 Paul, a servant of God, and an apostle of Jesus Christ, according to the faith of God's elect, and the acknowledging of the truth which is after godliness;

*2 Peter 1:3 According as his divine power hath given unto us all things that pertain unto life and godliness, through the knowledge of him that hath called us to glory and virtue:

*2 Peter 1:6 And to knowledge temperance; and to temperance patience; and to patience godliness;

*2 Peter 1:7 And to godliness brotherly kindness; and to brotherly kindness charity.

*2 Peter 3:11 Seeing then that all these things shall be dissolved, what manner of persons ought ye to be in all holy conversation and godliness,

*2 Timothy 3:12 - Yea, and all that will live godly in Christ Jesus shall suffer persecution.

*Psalms 1:1-3 - Blessed [is] the man that walketh not in the counsel of the ungodly, nor standeth in the way of sinners, nor sitteth in the seat of the scornful.

*Micah 6:8 - He hath shewed thee, O man, what [is] good; and what doth the LORD require of thee, but to do justly, and to love mercy, and to walk humbly with thy God?

*Jude 1:4 - For there are certain men crept in unawares, who were before of old ordained to this condemnation, ungodly men, turning the grace of our God into lasciviousness, and denying the only Lord God, and our Lord Jesus Christ.

*James 1:27 - Pure religion and undefiled before God and the Father is this, To visit the fatherless and widows in their affliction, [and] to keep himself unspotted from the world.

Brotherly Kindness

The quality of compassion and generosity, characteristic of God's dealings towards the weak and poor, and demanded of believers. The kindness is also shown in the words and deeds of Jesus Christ. Basically it means "doing thoughtful deeds to others."What is kindness? It is based on the mind-set described in:

*Philippians 2:3 Let nothing be done through strife or vainglory; but in lowliness of mind let each esteem other better than themselves.4 Look not every man on his own things, but every man also on the things of others.5 Let this mind be in you, which was also in Christ Jesus:

Kindness is humbly giving of ourselves in love and mercy to others who may not be able to give anything back, who sometimes don't deserve it, and who frequently don't thank us for it. Basically kindness means a way of thinking that leads to doing thoughtful deeds for others.

Ephesians 4:32 - And be ye kind one to another, tenderhearted, forgiving one another, even as God for Christ's sake hath forgiven you.

Luke 6:35 - But love ye your enemies, and do good, and lend, hoping for nothing again; and your reward shall be great, and ye shall be the children of the Highest: for he is kind unto the unthankful and [to] the evil.

Proverbs 11:17 - The merciful man doeth good to his own soul: but [he that is] cruel troubleth his own flesh.

Colossians 3:12 - Put on therefore, as the elect of God, holy and beloved, bowels of mercies, kindness, humbleness of mind, meekness, longsuffering;

Proverbs 31:26 - She openeth her mouth with wisdom; and in her tongue [is] the law of kindness.

1 Corinthians 13:4-7 - Charity suffereth long, [and] is kind; charity envieth not; charity vaunteth not itself, is not puffed up,   (Read More...)

Proverbs 19:17 - He that hath pity upon the poor lendeth unto the LORD; and that which he hath given will he pay him again.

Galatians 6:10 - As we have therefore opportunity, let us do good unto all [men], especially unto them who are of the household of faith.

1 Peter 3:9 - Not rendering evil for evil, or railing for railing: but contrariwise blessing; knowing that ye are thereunto called, that ye should inherit a blessing.

*Psalm 117:2 For his merciful kindness is great toward us: and the truth of the Lord endureth forever. Praise ye the Lord.

*Proverbs 19:22 The desire of a man is his kindness: and a poor man is better than a liar.

*2 Corinthians 6:6 By pureness, by knowledge, by long suffering, by kindness, by the Holy Ghost, by love unfeigned,

*Ephesians 2:7 That in the ages to come he might shew the exceeding riches of his grace in his kindness toward us through Christ Jesus.

*Titus 3:3 For we ourselves also were sometimes foolish, disobedient, deceived, serving divers lusts and pleasures, living in malice and envy, hateful, and hating one another.4 But after that the kindness and love of God our Saviour toward man appeared,5 Not by works of righteousness which we have done, but according to his mercy he saved us, by the washing of regeneration, and renewing of the Holy Ghost;

Charity

Charity is the word in the Bible for Divine Love! (Agape)True divine love is neither selfish nor insulated; where the love of God is in operation, bigotry does not exist, neither selfishness, disobedience to God, or immorality. "God Is Love. "Agape, the love revealed in the Bible, can only be expressed as the nature of God. John testifies that "God is love" (1 John 4:8). God does not merely love; he is love. Everything that God has, and does flows from His divine nature of love.

*1 Corinthians 13:1 Though I speak with the tongues of men and of angels, and have not charity, I am become as sounding brass, or a tinkling cymbal.

*1 Corinthians 13:4 Charity suffereth long, and is kind; charity envieth not; charity vaunteth not itself, is not puffed up,

*1 Corinthians 13:13 And now abideth faith, hope, charity, these three; but the greatest of these is charity.

*Colossians 3:14 And above all these things put on charity, which is the bond of perfectness.

*1 Timothy 1:5 Now the end of the commandment is charity out of a pure heart, and of a good conscience, and of faith unfeigned:

*1 Timothy 4:12 Let no man despise thy youth; but be thou an example of the believers, in word, in conversation, in charity, in spirit, in faith, in purity.

*2 Timothy 2:22 Flee also youthful lusts: but follow righteousness, faith, charity, peace, with them that call on the Lord out of a pure heart.

*2 Timothy 3:10 But thou hast fully known my doctrine, manner of life, purpose, faith, longsuffering, charity, patience,

*Titus 2:2 That the aged men be sober, grave, temperate, sound in faith, in charity, in patience.

*1 Peter 4:8 And above all things have fervent charity among yourselves: for charity shall cover the multitude of sins.

*Matthew 5:44 But I say unto you, Love your enemies, bless them that curse you, do good to them that hate you, and pray for them which despitefully use you, and persecute you;

*Matthew 22:37 Jesus said unto him, Thou shalt love the Lord thy God with all thy heart, and with all thy soul, and with all thy mind....

:39 And the second is like unto it, Thou shalt love thy neighbour as thyself.

*John 3:16 For God so loved the world, that he gave his only begotten Son, that whosoever believeth in him should not perish, but have everlasting life.

*John 13:34 A new commandment I give unto you, That ye love one another; as I have loved you, that ye also love one another.

*John 13:35 By this shall all men know that ye are my disciples, if ye have love one to another.

*John 14:15 If ye love me, keep my commandments.

*John 14:21 He that hath my commandments, and keepeth them, he it is that loveth me: and he that loveth me shall be loved of my Father, and I will love him, and will manifest myself to him.

*John 15:9 As the Father hath loved me, so have I loved you: continue ye in my love.

*John 15:10 If ye keep my commandments, ye shall abide in my love; even as I have kept my Father's commandments, and abide in his love.

*John 15:12 This is my commandment, That ye love one another, as I have loved you.

*John 17:23 I in them, and thou in me, that they may be made perfect in one; and that the world may know that thou hast sent me, and hast loved them, as thou hast loved me.

*Romans 5:5 And hope maketh not ashamed; because the love of God is shed abroad in our hearts by the Holy Ghost which is given unto us.

*Romans 5:8 But God commendeth his love toward us, in that, while we were yet sinners, Christ died for us.

*Romans 8:28 And we know that all things work together for good to them that love God, to them who are the called according to his purpose.

*1 Corinthians 2:9 But as it is written, Eye hath not seen, nor ear heard, neither have entered into the heart of man, the things which God hath prepared for them that love him.

---

*2 Corinthians 5:14 For the love of Christ constraineth us; because we thus judge, that if one died for all, then were all dead:

---

*2 Corinthians 6:6 By pureness, by knowledge, by long suffering, by kindness, by the Holy Ghost, by love unfeigned,

---

*Galatians 5:6 For in Jesus Christ neither circumcision availeth anything, nor uncircumcision; but faith which worketh by love.

---

*Galatians 5:14 For all the law is fulfilled in one word, even in this; Thou shalt love thy neighbor as thyself.

---

*Ephesians 3:17 That Christ may dwell in your hearts by faith; that ye, being rooted and grounded in love,

---

*Ephesians 3:19 And to know the love of Christ, which passeth knowledge, that ye might be filled with all the fulness of God.

---

*Ephesians 4:15 But speaking the truth in love, may grow up into him in all things, which is the head, even Christ:

---

*Philippians 2:1 If there be therefore any consolation in Christ, if any comfort of love, if any fellowship of the Spirit, if any bowels and mercies,

---

*1 Thessalonians 3:12 And the Lord make you to increase and abound in love one toward another, and toward all men, even as we do toward you:

---

*2 Timothy 1:7 For God hath not given us the spirit of fear; but of power, and of love, and of a sound mind.

---

*1 Timothy 6:11 But thou, O man of God, flee these things; and follow after righteousness, godliness, faith, love, patience, meekness.

*James 1:12 Blessed is the man that endureth temptation: for when he is tried, he shall receive the crown of life, which the Lord hath promised to them that love him.

*James 2:5 Hearken, my beloved brethren, Hath not God chosen the poor of this world rich in faith, and heirs of the kingdom which he hath promised to them that love him?

*1 Peter 1:22 Seeing ye have purified your souls in obeying the truth through the Spirit unto unfeigned love of the brethren, see that ye love one another with a pure heart fervently:

*1 Peter 3:8 Finally, be ye all of one mind, having compassion one of another, love as brethren, be pitiful, be courteous:

*1 John 3:14 We know that we have passed from death unto life, because we love the brethren. He that loveth not his brother abideth in death.

*1 John 3:16 Hereby perceive we the love of God, because he laid down his life for us: and we ought to lay down our lives for the brethren.

*1 John 3:18 My little children, let us not love in word, neither in tongue; but indeed and in truth.

*1 John 4:7 Beloved, let us love one another: for love is of God; and every one that loveth is born of God, and knoweth God. 8 He that loveth not knoweth not God; for God is love.

*1 John 4:16 And we have known and believed the love that God hath to us. God is love; and he that dwelleth in love dwelleth in God, and God in him.

*1 John 5:3 For this is the love of God, that we keep his commandments: and his commandments are not grievous.

JOY

The words joy, rejoice are the most words used to translate the Hebrew and Greek words pertaining to JOY in the English bible. Joy is found over 150 times in the Bible, and with the words "joyous" and "joyful" included, the number comes to over 200. The word rejoice appears over 200 times. Now joy is a fruit, a manifestation of the Spirit in a believers life. Joy is not based on circumstances, feelings, natural events, or conditions of life. Joy is not like happiness which is based upon happenings, or if everything is going well, or if it is not going well. Divine joy is based upon, and comes from nothing but faith, trust, confidence in God, and His word, His Promises. Joy is the anticipation, the expectation of what God has promised, and its fulfillment! It could be described as exhilaration, delight, extreme gladness, and excitement.

*Psalm 16:11 Thou wilt shew me the path of life: in thy presence is fulness of joy; at thy right hand there are pleasures for evermore.

*Romans 12:12 - Rejoicing in hope; patient in tribulation; continuing instant in prayer;

*James 1:2 - My brethren, count it all joy when ye fall into divers temptations;

*Nehemiah 8:10 ...: neither be ye sorry; for the joy of the Lord is your strength.

*Philippians 4:4 - Rejoice in the Lord alway: [and] again I say, Rejoice.

*Romans 15:13 - Now the God of hope fill you with all joy and peace in believing, that ye may abound in hope, through the power of the Holy Ghost.

*Galatians 5:22 - But the fruit of the Spirit is love, joy, peace, longsuffering, gentleness, goodness, faith,

*John 16:24 - Hitherto have ye asked nothing in my name: ask, and ye shall receive, that your joy may be full.

*1 Peter 1:8 - Whom having not seen, ye love; in whom, though now ye see [him] not, yet believing, ye rejoice with joy unspeakable and full of glory:

*Proverbs 17:22 - A merry heart doeth good [like] a medicine: but a broken spirit drieth the bones.

*Romans 14:17 - For the kingdom of God is not meat and drink; but righteousness, and peace, and joy in the Holy Ghost.

*John 16:22 - And ye now therefore have sorrow: but I will see you again, and your heart shall rejoice, and your joy no man taketh from you.

*James 1:2-4 - My brethren, count it all joy when ye fall into divers temptations;   (Read More...)

*Psalms 16:9 - Therefore my heart is glad, and my glory rejoiceth: my flesh also shall rest in hope.

*1 Thessalonians 5:16 - Rejoice evermore.

*Psalm 32:11 Be glad in the Lord, and rejoice, ye righteous: and shout for joy, all ye that are upright in heart.

*Psalm 35:9 And my soul shall be joyful in the Lord: it shall rejoice in his salvation.

*Psalm 35:27 Let them shout for joy, and be glad, that favour my righteous cause: yea, let them say continually, Let the Lord be magnified, which hath pleasure in the prosperity of his servant.

*Psalm 51:12 Restore unto me the joy of thy salvation; and uphold me with thy free spirit.

*Psalm 98:4 Make a joyful noise unto the Lord, all the earth: make a loud noise, and rejoice, and sing praise.

*Psalm 105:43 And he brought forth his people with joy, and his chosen with gladness:

CHAPTER SEVEN

Goodness

Gods goodness is a declaration of his character, His very nature. It is His benevolence; towards humanity, it is mercy, pity, compassion, in his dealing with sinners, long-suffering patience. "God's goodness appears in two realities, in His giving and forgiving. "God, by nature is absolutely good, as revealed in:

Psalm 34:8 tells us: "Taste and see that the LORD is good; blessed is the one who takes refuge in him."

He is the foundation of goodness and of everything that is good, or ever will be good! All goodness comes from God, and Him alone.

*Exodus 34:6 And the Lord passed by before him, and proclaimed, The Lord, The Lord God, merciful and gracious, longsuffering, and abundant in goodness and truth,

*Romans 2:4 Or despisest thou the riches of his goodness and forbearance and longsuffering; not knowing that the goodness of God leadeth thee to repentance?

*Mark 10:18 And Jesus said unto him, Why callest thou me good? there is none good but one, that is, God.

*Romans 8:28 - And we know that all things work together for good to them that love God, to them who are the called according to [his] purpose.

*Psalms 23:6 - Surely goodness and mercy shall follow me all the days of my life: and I will dwell in the house of the LORD forever.

*Psalms 31:19 - [Oh] how great [is] thy goodness, which thou hast laid up for them that fear thee; [which] thou hast wrought for them that trust in thee before the sons of men!

*Psalm 33:5 He loveth righteousness and judgment: the earth is full of the goodness of the Lord.

*Galatians 5:22-23 - But the fruit of the Spirit is love, joy, peace, longsuffering, gentleness, goodness, faith,   (Read More...)

*Romans 12:9 - [Let] love be without dissimulation. Abhor that which is evil; cleave to that which is good.

*Galatians 5:22 - But the fruit of the Spirit is love, joy, peace, longsuffering, gentleness, goodness, faith,

*Psalms 27:13 - [I had fainted], unless I had believed to see the goodness of the LORD in the land of the living.

*James 3:13 - Who [is] a wise man and endued with knowledge among you? let him shew out of a good conversation his works with meekness of wisdom.

*James 1:17 - Every good gift and every perfect gift is from above, and cometh down from the Father of lights, with whom is no variableness, neither shadow of turning.

*Galatians 6:10 - As we have therefore opportunity, let us do good unto all [men], especially unto them who are of the household of faith.

*Ephesians 5:9 (For the fruit of the Spirit is in all goodness and righteousness and truth;)

*Psalms 34:8 - O taste and see that the LORD [is] good: blessed [is] the man [that] trusteth in him.

*Micah 6:8 - He hath shewed thee, O man, what [is] good; and what doth the LORD require of thee, but to do justly, and to love mercy, and to walk humbly with thy God?

*Psalms 25:7 - Remember not the sins of my youth, nor my transgressions: according to thy mercy remember thou me for thy goodness' sake, O LORD.

---

*Matthew 12:35 - A good man out of the good treasure of the heart bringeth forth good things: and an evil man out of the evil treasure bringeth forth evil things.

---

*Titus 3:8-10 - [This is] a faithful saying, and these things I will that thou affirm constantly, that they which have believed in God might be careful to maintain good works. These things are good and profitable unto men.

---

*Psalm 107:8 Oh that men would praise the Lord for his goodness, and for his wonderful works to the children of men! :9 For he satisfieth the longing soul, and filleth the hungry soul with goodness.

Meekness

A definition of biblical meekness is = **Strength under control**. Just as Jesus who was all-powerful took upon himself the form of a servant, and was obedient to His Father, even unto death, so Christ has called us to be meek as he was, and is. It means to be Mild of temper; gentle; not easily provoked or irritated; yielding; given to forbearance under injuries.

True humility; submits to the divine will of God; not proud, self-sufficient or self-seeking, or self-serving; not apt to complain, or murmur. MEE'KNESS, n. Softness of temper; mildness; gentleness; forbearance under injuries and provocations. Let us look at the first four beatitudes in Matthew 5:

1. **"Blessed are the poor in spirit"** - Those who recognize their spiritual poverty. They understand that they are powerless to save themselves, and there righteousness is as filthy rags.

2. **"Blessed are they that mourn"** - They not only realizes that they are sinners, are lost, but that they are also powerless to save themselves, and act upon that knowledge in grieving over their sinful, and lost condition. Not only do they mourn for themselves, but all of humanity.

3. **"Blessed are the meek"** - These are they who understand their spiritual poverty, mourn over their lost condition and are willing to submit their lives completely over to the will of God, his word, and his nature.

4. **"Blessed are they that hunger and thirst after righteousness"** - They hunger and thirst to be just like their heavenly Father in nature, Character, Attitude, and Disposition!

*Matthew 5:5 - Blessed [are] the meek: for they shall inherit the earth.

*Titus 3:2 - To speak evil of no man, to be no brawlers, [but] gentle, shewing all meekness unto all men.

*Matthew 11:29 - Take my yoke upon you, and learn of me; for I am meek and lowly in heart: and ye shall find rest unto your souls.

*Numbers 12:3 (Now the man Moses was very meek, above all the men which were upon the face of the earth.)

*Psalm 22:26 The meek shall eat and be satisfied: they shall praise the Lord that seek him: your heart shall live for ever.

*Psalm 25:9 The meek will he guide in judgment: and the meek will he teach his way.

*Psalm 37:11 But the meek shall inherit the earth; and shall delight themselves in the abundance of peace.

*Psalm 45:4 And in thy majesty ride prosperously because of truth and meekness and righteousness; and thy right hand shall teach thee terrible things.

*Psalm 76:9 When God arose to judgment, to save all the meek of the earth. Selah.

*Psalm 147:6 The Lord lifteth up the meek: he casteth the wicked down to the ground.

*Psalm 149:4 For the Lord taketh pleasure in his people: he will beautify the meek with salvation.

---

*James 3:13 - Who [is] a wise man and endued with knowledge among you? let him shew out of a good conversation his works with meekness of wisdom.

---

*1 Peter 3:4 - But [let it be] the hidden man of the heart, in that which is not corruptible, [even the ornament] of a meek and quiet spirit, which is in the sight of God of great price.

---

*Numbers 12:3 - (Now the man Moses [was] very meek, above all the men which [were] upon the face of the earth.)

---

*1 Peter 3:15 - But sanctify the Lord God in your hearts: and [be] ready always to [give] an answer to every man that asketh you a reason of the hope that is in you with meekness and fear:

---

*Romans 12:14 - Bless them which persecute you: bless, and curse not.

---

*Isaiah 29:19 The meek also shall increase their joy in the Lord, and the poor among men shall rejoice in the Holy One of Israel.

---

*Zephaniah 2:3 Seek ye the Lord, all ye meek of the earth, which have wrought his judgment; seek righteousness, seek meekness: it may be ye shall be hid in the day of the Lord's anger.

---

*2 Corinthians 10:1 Now I Paul myself beseech you by the meekness and gentleness of Christ,

---

*Galatians 6:1 Brethren, if a man be overtaken in a fault, ye which are spiritual, restore such an one in the spirit of meekness; considering thyself, lest thou also be tempted.

---

*Ephesians 4:2 With all lowliness and meekness, with longsuffering, forbearing one another in love;

---

*James 1:21 Wherefore lay apart all filthiness and superfluity of naughtiness, and receive with meekness the engrafted word, which is able to

save your souls.

Peace Makers

PEACE = In a general sense, a state of divine quiet or tranquillity; freedom from disturbance or agitation; in spirit, soul, mind, or emotions. It is freedom from agitation or disturbance by the passions, as from fear, terror, anger, anxiety or the like; quietness of mind; tranquillity; calmness; quiet of conscience. Freedom from mental perturbation; as peacefulness of mind.

*Psalm 119:165 Great peace have they which love thy law: and nothing shall offend them.

Heavenly rest; the happiness of heaven. Harmony; concord; a state of reconciliation between parties at variance. This word is used in silence or quiet; to the troubled soul. To be at peace, to be reconciled; to live in harmony.

Peacemaker = One who makes peace by reconciling parties that are at variance.

*Matthew 5:9 Blessed are the peacemakers: for they shall be called the children of God.

*Philippians 4:6 - Be careful for nothing; but in everything by prayer and supplication with thanksgiving let your requests be made known unto God. 7 And the peace of God, which passeth all understanding, shall keep your hearts and minds through Christ Jesus.

*2 Thessalonians 3:16 - Now the Lord of peace himself give you peace always by all means. The Lord [be] with you all.

*John 16:33 - These things I have spoken unto you, that in me ye might have peace. In the world ye shall have tribulation: but be of good cheer; I have overcome the world.

*Isaiah 26:3 - Thou wilt keep [him] in perfect peace, [whose] mind [is] stayed [on thee]: because he trusteth in thee.

*1 Peter 5:7 - Casting all your care upon him; for he careth for you.

*Romans 12:18 - If it be possible, as much as lieth in you, live peaceably with all men.

*1 Peter 3:11 - Let him eschew evil, and do good; let him seek peace, and ensue it.

*Romans 15:13 - Now the God of hope fill you with all joy and peace in believing, that ye may abound in hope, through the power of the Holy Ghost.

*1 Corinthians 14:33 - For God is not [the author] of confusion, but of peace, as in all churches of the saints.

*Isaiah 12:2 - Behold, God [is] my salvation; I will trust, and not be afraid: for the LORD JEHOVAH [is] my strength and [my] song; he also is become my salvation.

*Psalm 29:11 The Lord will give strength unto his people; the Lord will bless his people with peace.

*Psalm 34:14 Depart from evil, and do good; seek peace, and pursue it.

*Psalm 85:8 I will hear what God the Lord will speak: for he will speak peace unto his people, and to his saints: but let them not turn again to folly.

*Psalm 85:10 Mercy and truth are met together; righteousness and peace have kissed each other.

*Colossians 3:15 And let the peace of God rule in your hearts, to the which also ye are called in one body; and be ye thankful.

*Ephesians 2:14 For he is our peace, who hath made both one, and hath broken down the middle wall of partition between us;

*Ephesians 2:17 And came and preached peace to you which were afar off, and to them that were nigh.

*Ephesians 4:3 Endeavouring to keep the unity of the Spirit in the bond of peace.

Longsuffering

It means to endure injuries, abuses, afflictions, wrongs done for a very long time; without responding with retribution!

*Exodus 34:6 - And the LORD passed by before him, and proclaimed, The LORD, The LORD God, merciful and gracious, longsuffering, and abundant in goodness and truth,

*Numbers 14:18 The Lord is longsuffering, and of great mercy, forgiving iniquity and transgression, and by no means clearing the guilty, visiting the iniquity of the fathers upon the children unto the third and fourth generation.

*2 Peter 3:9 - The Lord is not slack concerning his promise, as some men count slackness; but is longsuffering to us-ward, not willing that any should perish, but that all should come to repentance.

*Ephesians 4:2 - With all lowliness and meekness, with longsuffering, forbearing one another in love;

*Romans 8:28 - And we know that all things work together for good to them that love God, to them who are the called according to [his] purpose.

*Galatians 5:22 - But the fruit of the Spirit is love, joy, peace, longsuffering, gentleness, goodness, faith,

*James 4:7 - Submit yourselves therefore to God. Resist the devil, and he will flee from you.

*Romans 2:4 - Or despisest thou the riches of his goodness and forbearance and longsuffering; not knowing that the goodness of God leadeth thee to repentance?

---

*Hebrews 2:10 - For it became him, for whom [are] all things, and by whom [are] all things, in bringing many sons unto glory, to make the captain of their salvation perfect through sufferings.

---

*Romans 9:22 - [What] if God, willing to shew [his] wrath, and to make his power known, endured with much longsuffering the vessels of wrath fitted to destruction:

---

*Romans 5:3-4 - And not only [so], but we glory in tribulations also: knowing that tribulation worketh patience;

---

*Colossians 3:12 Put on therefore, as the elect of God, holy and beloved, bowels of mercies, kindness, humbleness of mind, meekness, longsuffering;

---

*1 Timothy 1:16 Howbeit for this cause I obtained mercy, that in me first Jesus Christ might shew forth all longsuffering, for a pattern to them which should hereafter believe on him to life everlasting.

---

*2 Timothy 3:10 But thou hast fully known my doctrine, manner of life, purpose, faith, longsuffering, charity, patience,

---

*1 Peter 3:20 Which sometime were disobedient, when once the longsuffering of God waited in the days of Noah, while the ark was a preparing, wherein few, that is, eight souls were saved by water.

---

*2 Peter 3:15 And account that the longsuffering of our Lord is salvation; even as our beloved brother Paul also according to the wisdom given unto him hath written unto you;

Gentleness

To be nonabrasive, soft, soothing, tender, calm, serene, tranquil; easy, sweetness of disposition, lenient, merciful. Without violence, roughness or asperity.

*Titus 3:2 - To speak evil of no man, to be no brawlers, [but] gentle, shewing all meekness unto all men.

*1 Peter 3:15 - But sanctify the Lord God in your hearts: and [be] ready always to [give] an answer to every man that asketh you a reason of the hope that is in you with meekness and fear:

*Psalms 18:35 - Thou hast also given me the shield of thy salvation: and thy right hand hath holden me up, and thy gentleness hath made me great.

*2 Timothy 2:24-26 - And the servant of the Lord must not strive; but be gentle unto all [men], apt to teach, patient, (Read More...)

*James 3:17 - But the wisdom that is from above is first pure, then peaceable, gentle, [and] easy to be intreated, full of mercy and good fruits, without partiality, and without hypocrisy.

*Galatians 6:1 - Brethren, if a man be overtaken in a fault, ye which are spiritual, restore such an one in the spirit of meekness; considering thyself, lest thou also be tempted.

*Proverbs 15:1 - A soft answer turneth away wrath: but grievous words stir up anger.

*Matthew 11:29 - Take my yoke upon you, and learn of me; for I am meek and lowly in heart: and ye shall find rest unto your souls.

*James 1:19-20 - Wherefore, my beloved brethren, let every man be swift to hear, slow to speak, slow to wrath:

*2 Samuel 22:36 - Thou hast also given me the shield of thy salvation: and thy gentleness hath made me great.

*1 Corinthians 13:4-5 - Charity suffereth long, [and] is kind; charity envieth not; charity vaunteth not itself, is not puffed up,

*Ephesians 4:2 - With all lowliness and meekness, with longsuffering, forbearing one another in love;

*1 Thessalonians 2:7 - But we were gentle among you, even as a nurse cherisheth her children:

*Galatians 5:22 - But the fruit of the Spirit is love, joy, peace, longsuffering, gentleness, goodness, faith,

*Isaiah 40:11 - He shall feed his flock like a shepherd: he shall gather the lambs with his arm, and carry [them] in his bosom, [and] shall gently lead those that are with young.

Holiness

The state of being holy; it means purity or integrity of moral character; freedom from sin; sanctity. Applied to the nature of God, holiness denotes perfect purity or integrity of moral character.

*Exodus 15:11 Who is like unto thee, O Lord, among the gods? who is like thee, glorious in holiness, fearful in praises, doing wonders?

When it comes to believers it is purity of heart or dispositions; sanctified affections; piety; moral goodness. That which is separated to the service of God. We call a man holy, when his heart is conformed in some degree to the image of God, and his life is regulated by the divine precepts. Hence, holy is used as nearly synonymous with good, pious, godly.

*Jeremiah 2:3Israel was holiness unto the Lord, and the firstfruits of his increase:

Hallowed; consecrated or set apart to a sacred use, or to the service or worship of God; a sense frequent in Scripture; as the holy sabbath; holy oil; holy vessels; a holy nation; the holy temple; a holy priesthood.

*2 Corinthians 7:1 - Having therefore these promises, dearly beloved, let us cleanse ourselves from all filthiness of the flesh and spirit, perfecting holiness in the fear of God.

*1 Thessalonians 4:7 - For God hath not called us unto uncleanness, but unto holiness.

*Hebrews 12:14 - Follow peace with all [men], and holiness, without which no man shall see the Lord:

*Leviticus 19:2 - Speak unto all the congregation of the children of Israel, and say unto them, Ye shall be holy: for I the LORD your God [am] holy.

*Leviticus 20:26 - And ye shall be holy unto me: for I the LORD [am] holy, and have severed you from [other] people, that ye should be mine.

*Isaiah 35:8 - And an highway shall be there, and a way, and it shall be called The way of holiness; the unclean shall not pass over it; but it [shall be] for those: the wayfaring men, though fools, shall not err [therein].

*1 Thessalonians 5:23 - And the very God of peace sanctify you wholly; and [I pray God] your whole spirit and soul and body be preserved blameless unto the coming of our Lord Jesus Christ.

*James 1:21 - Wherefore lay apart all filthiness and superfluity of naughtiness, and receive with meekness the engrafted word, which is able to save your souls.

*1 John 3:3 - And every man that hath this hope in him purifieth himself, even as he is pure.

*Hebrews 12:10 - For they verily for a few days chastened [us] after their own pleasure; but he for [our] profit, that [we] might be partakers of his holiness.

*1 Corinthians 15:34 - Awake to righteousness, and sin not; for some have not the knowledge of God: I speak [this] to your shame.

*1 Corinthians 6:20 - For ye are bought with a price: therefore glorify God in your body, and in your spirit, which are God's.

*1 John 1:7 - But if we walk in the light, as he is in the light, we have fellowship one with another, and the blood of Jesus Christ his Son cleanseth us from all sin.

*1 Timothy 6:6 - But godliness with contentment is great gain.

*Matthew 5:8 - Blessed [are] the pure in heart: for they shall see God.

*Matthew 5:6 - Blessed [are] they which do hunger and thirst after righteousness: for they shall be filled.

Mercy

Being compassionate; tender towards offenders, and to forgive their offenses; unwilling to punish for injuries; **Exodus 34:6 And the Lord passed by before him, and proclaimed, The Lord, The Lord God, merciful and gracious, longsuffering, and abundant in goodness and truth.** A willingness to forbear punishment; readiness to forgive. That benevolence, mildness or tenderness of heart which causes a person to overlook injuries, or to treat an offender better than he deserves; to inflict less than law or justice should demand. It implies benevolence, tenderness, mildness, pity or compassion, and clemency, but exercised only towards offenders. Mercy is a distinguishing attribute of God.

I*Luke 6:36 - Be ye therefore merciful, as your Father also is merciful.

*James 2:13 - For he shall have judgment without mercy, that hath shewed no mercy; and mercy rejoiceth against judgment.

*Matthew 5:7 - Blessed [are] the merciful: for they shall obtain mercy.

*1 John 1:9 - If we confess our sins, he is faithful and just to forgive us [our] sins, and to cleanse us from all unrighteousness.

*Matthew 9:13 - But go ye and learn what [that] meaneth, I will have mercy, and not sacrifice: for I am not come to call the righteous, but sinners to repentance.

*1 Peter 1:3 - Blessed [be] the God and Father of our Lord Jesus Christ, which according to his abundant mercy hath begotten us again unto a lively hope by the resurrection of Jesus Christ from the dead,

*Hebrews 4:16 - Let us therefore come boldly unto the throne of grace, that we may obtain mercy, and find grace to help in time of need.

*Colossians 3:12 - Put on therefore, as the elect of God, holy and beloved, bowels of mercies, kindness, humbleness of mind, meekness, longsuffering;

*Luke 6:37 - Judge not, and ye shall not be judged: condemn not, and ye shall not be condemned: forgive, and ye shall be forgiven:

*James 2:12 So speak ye, and so do, as they that shall be judged by the law of liberty. 13 For he shall have judgment without mercy, that hath shewed no mercy; and mercy rejoiceth against judgment.

*Colossians 3:13 - Forbearing one another, and forgiving one another, if any man have a quarrel against any: even as Christ forgave you, so also [do] ye.

*Jude 1:23-25 - And others save with fear, pulling [them] out of the fire; hating even the garment spotted by the flesh.

*1 Corinthians 10:13 - There hath no temptation taken you but such as is common to man: but God [is] faithful, who will not suffer you to be tempted above that ye are able; but will with the temptation also make a way to escape, that ye may be able to bear [it].

*Proverbs 14:21 - He that despiseth his neighbour sinneth: but he that hath mercy on the poor, happy [is] he.

*Micah 6:8 - He hath shewed thee, O man, what [is] good; and what doth the LORD require of thee, but to do justly, and to love mercy, and to walk humbly with thy God?

Reverence

This holy fear is more than reverence, or awe! In the scriptures it is described as "terror," or "dread."

*Philippians 2:12 Wherefore, my beloved, as ye have always obeyed, not as in my presence only, but now much more in my absence, work out your own salvation with fear and trembling.

*Proverbs 8:13 - The fear of the LORD [is] to hate evil: pride, and arrogancy, and the evil way, and the froward mouth, do I hate.

*2 Corinthians 5:11 Knowing therefore the terror of the Lord, we persuade men; but we are made manifest unto God; and I trust also are made manifest in your consciences.

*Isaiah 8:13 Sanctify the Lord of hosts himself; and let him be your fear, and let him be your dread.

*Proverbs 1:7 - The fear of the LORD [is] the beginning of knowledge:

*Matthew 10:28 - And fear not them which kill the body, but are not able to kill the soul: but rather fear him which is able to destroy both soul and body in hell.

*Psalms 33:8 - Let all the earth fear the LORD: let all the inhabitants of the world stand in awe of him.

*Proverbs 14:27 - The fear of the LORD [is] a fountain of life, to depart from the snares of death.

*Psalms 25:14 - The secret of the LORD [is] with them that fear him; and he will shew them his covenant.

---

*Deuteronomy 10:12 - And now, Israel, what doth the LORD thy God require of thee, but to fear the LORD thy God, to walk in all his ways, and to love him, and to serve the LORD thy God with all thy heart and with all thy soul,

---

*Proverbs 16:6 - By mercy and truth iniquity is purged: and by the fear of the LORD [men] depart from evil.

---

*Psalms 19:9 - The fear of the LORD [is] clean, enduring forever: the judgments of the LORD [are] true [and] righteous altogether.

---

*1 Peter 1:17 - And if ye call on the Father, who without respect of persons judgeth according to every man's work, pass the time of your sojourning [here] in fear:

---

*Ephesians 5:21 - Submitting yourselves one to another in the fear of God.

---

*Proverbs 14:16 - A wise [man] feareth, and departeth from evil: but the fool rageth, and is confident.

---

*Ecclesiastes 12:13 - Let us hear the conclusion of the whole matter: Fear God, and keep his commandments: for this [is] the whole [duty] of man.

---

*Job 28:28 - And unto man he said, Behold, the fear of the Lord, that [is] wisdom; and to depart from evil [is] understanding.

---

*Proverbs 3:7 - Be not wise in thine own eyes: fear the LORD, and depart from evil.

CHAPTER EIGHT

Offensive Weapons

To take the initiative by beginning to attack or act aggressively towards the opposition. "security forces took the offensive ten days ago" synonyms: launch an attack, begin to attack, attack first, strike the first blow "our fleet will take the offensive within the next 48 hours" Related to go on the offensive: take the offensive, goes on the offensive, took the offensive.

Having a Vision

*Proverbs 29:18 Where there is no vision, the people perish: but he that keepeth the law, happy is he.

*Psalm 119:2 Blessed are they that keep his testimonies, and that seek him with the whole heart.

*Psalm 31:24 Be of good courage, and he shall strengthen your heart, all ye that hope in the Lord.

*Psalm 33:18 Behold, the eye of the Lord is upon them that fear him, upon them that hope in his mercy;

*Psalm 38:15 For in thee, O Lord, do I hope: thou wilt hear, O Lord my God.

*Psalm 39:7 And now, Lord, what wait I for? my hope is in thee.

*Psalm 71:5 For thou art my hope, O Lord God: thou art my trust from my youth.

*Psalm 71:14 But I will hope continually, and will yet praise thee more and more.

*Psalm 119:114 Thou art my hiding place and my shield: I hope in thy word.

*Psalm 130:5 I wait for the Lord, my soul doth wait, and in his word do I hope.

*Proverbs 10:28 The hope of the righteous shall be gladness: but the expectation of the wicked shall perish.

*Proverbs 13:12 Hope deferred maketh the heart sick: but when the desire cometh, it is a tree of life.

*Romans 4:18 Who against hope believed in hope, that he might become the father of many nations, according to that which was spoken, So shall thy seed be.

*Romans 5:4 And patience, experience; and experience, hope:5 And hope maketh not ashamed; because the love of God is shed abroad in our hearts by the Holy Ghost which is given unto us.

*Romans 8:24 For we are saved by hope: but hope that is seen is not hope: for what a man seeth, why doth he yet hope for? :25 But if we hope for that we see not, then do we with patience wait for it.

*Romans 15:13 Now the God of hope fill you with all joy and peace in believing, that ye may abound in hope, through the power of the Holy Ghost.

*Colossians 1:27 To whom God would make known what is the riches of the glory of this mystery among the Gentiles; which is Christ in you, the hope of glory:

*1 Thessalonians 5:8 But let us, who are of the day, be sober, putting on the breastplate of faith and love; and for an helmet, the hope of salvation.

*Titus 1:2 In hope of eternal life, which God, that cannot lie, promised before the world began;

*Titus 2:13 Looking for that blessed hope, and the glorious appearing of the great God and our Saviour Jesus Christ;

*Hebrews 6:19 Which hope we have as an anchor of the soul, both sure and stedfast, and which entereth into that within the veil;

*Hebrews 11:1 Now faith is the substance of things hoped for, the evidence of things not seen.

*1 Peter 1:21 Who by him do believe in God, that raised him up from the dead, and gave him glory; that your faith and hope might be in God.

*1 John 3:2 Beloved, now are we the sons of God, and it doth not yet appear what we shall be: but we know that, when he shall appear, we shall be like him; for we shall see him as he is.3 And every man that hath this hope in him purifieth himself, even as he is pure.4 Whosoever committeth sin transgresseth also the law: for sin is the transgression of the law.

Knowing Your Purpose

*Matthew 4:19 And he saith unto them, Follow me, and I will make you fishers of men.

*Jeremiah 1:5 Before I formed thee in the belly I knew thee; and before thou camest forth out of the womb I sanctified thee, and I ordained thee a prophet unto the nations.

*Philippians 3:14 I press toward the mark for the prize of the high calling of God in Christ Jesus.

*1 Peter 5:2 feed the flock of God which is among you, taking the oversight thereof, not by constraint, but willingly; not for filthy lucre, but of a ready mind;

*2 Timothy 4:2 preach the word; be instant in season, out of season; reprove, rebuke, exhort with all longsuffering and doctrine.

*1 Corinthians 7:20 Let every man abide in the same calling wherein he was called.

*John 15:16 Ye have not chosen me, but I have chosen you, and ordained you, that ye should go and bring forth fruit, and that your fruit should remain: that whatsoever ye shall ask of the Father in my name, he may give it you.

*1 Peter 4:11 If any man speak, let him speak as the oracles of God; if any man minister, let him do it as of the ability which God giveth: that God in all things may be glorified through Jesus Christ, to whom be praise and dominion for ever and ever. Amen.

*Ephesians 1:4 - According as he hath chosen us in him before the foundation of the world, that we should be holy and without blame before him in love:

*Colossians 2:9 - For in him dwelleth all the fulness of the Godhead bodily.

*Ephesians 4:1-15 - I therefore, the prisoner of the Lord, beseech you that ye walk worthy of the vocation wherewith ye are called,

*1 Corinthians 6:19-20 - What? know ye not that your body is the temple of the Holy Ghost [which is] in you, which ye have of God, and ye are not your own?

*Matthew 6:19-21 - Lay not up for yourselves treasures upon earth, where moth and rust doth corrupt, and where thieves break through and steal:

*Galatians 2:20 - I am crucified with Christ: nevertheless I live; yet not I, but Christ liveth in me: and the life which I now live in the flesh I live by the faith of the Son of God, who loved me, and gave himself for me.

---

*Luke 16:13 - No servant can serve two masters: for either he will hate the one, and love the other; or else he will hold to the one, and despise the other. Ye cannot serve God and mammon.

---

*Mark 16:16 - He that believeth and is baptized shall be saved; but he that believeth not shall be damned.

---

*Genesis 1:27 - So God created man in his [own] image, in the image of God created he him; male and female created he them.

---

*Romans 12:4 - For as we have many members in one body, and all members have not the same office:

---

*Jeremiah 29:11 - For I know the thoughts that I think toward you, saith the LORD, thoughts of peace, and not of evil, to give you an expected end.

---

*John 14:6 - Jesus saith unto him, I am the way, the truth, and the life: no man cometh unto the Father, but by me.

---

*1 Peter 2:9 - But ye [are] a chosen generation, a royal priesthood, an holy nation, a peculiar people; that ye should shew forth the praises of him who hath called you out of darkness into his marvellous light:

---

*Colossians 1:16 - For by him were all things created, that are in heaven, and that are in earth, visible and invisible, whether [they be] thrones, or dominions, or principalities, or powers: all things were created by him, and for him:

---

*Matthew 28:18-20 - And Jesus came and spake unto them, saying, All power is given unto me in heaven and in earth.

---

*Isaiah 46:10 - Declaring the end from the beginning, and from ancient times [the things] that are not [yet] done, saying, My counsel shall stand, and I will do all my pleasure:

*Revelation 4:11 - Thou art worthy, O Lord, to receive glory and honour and power: for thou hast created all things, and for thy pleasure they are and were created.

Walking In The Spirit

In order to walk in the spirit we must be full of the word of God. The divine influence of the Holy Spirit must have complete possession of our lives. There are many scriptures that deal with his particular subject of living, moving, operating, and flowing in the Holy Ghost. God is looking for those who will be completely yielded and surrendered to him in all areas of their life. when we walk in the spirit we will not fulfill the lust of the flesh. Meditate upon these realities and you will soon begin to see wonderful and amazing transformation in all that you do and say. When you walk in the spirit the fruits of the spirit will be manifested in your life.

*Galatians 5:16 This I say then, Walk in the Spirit, and ye shall not fulfil the lust of the flesh. 17 For the flesh lusteth against the Spirit, and the Spirit against the flesh: and these are contrary the one to the other: so that ye cannot do the things that ye would.

*Galatians 5:24 And they that are Christ's have crucified the flesh with the affections and lusts. 25 If we live in the Spirit, let us also walk in the Spirit. 26 Let us not be desirous of vain glory, provoking one another, envying one another.

*1 Peter 2:11 Dearly beloved, I beseech you as strangers and pilgrims, abstain from fleshly lusts, which war against the soul;

*Romans 8:12 Therefore, brethren, we are debtors, not to the flesh, to live after the flesh.13 For if ye live after the flesh, ye shall die: but if ye through the Spirit do mortify the deeds of the body, ye shall live.14 For as many as are led by the Spirit of God, they are the sons of God.

*Colossians 3:9 Lie not one to another, seeing that ye have put off the old man with his deeds;10 And have put on the new man, which is renewed in knowledge after the image of him that created him:

*Deuteronomy 8:6 Therefore thou shalt keep the commandments of the Lord thy God, to walk in his ways, and to fear him.

*Romans 8:1 There is therefore now no condemnation to them which are in Christ Jesus, who walk not after the flesh, but after the Spirit. 2 For the law of the Spirit of life in Christ Jesus hath made me free from the law of sin and death. 3 For what the law could not do, in that it was weak through the flesh, God sending his own Son in the likeness of sinful flesh, and for sin, condemned sin in the flesh:

*Colossians 1:10 that ye might walk worthy of the Lord unto all pleasing, being fruitful in every good work, and increasing in the knowledge of God;

*1 Thessalonians 2:12 that ye would walk worthy of God, who hath called you unto his kingdom and glory.

*2 Corinthians 5:7 (for we walk by faith, not by sight)

*Romans 1:17 For therein is the righteousness of God revealed from faith to faith: as it is written, The just shall live by faith.

*Galatians 2:20 I am crucified with Christ: nevertheless I live; yet not I, but Christ liveth in me: and the life which I now live in the flesh I live by the faith of the Son of God, who loved me, and gave himself for me.

*Galatians 3:11 But that no man is justified by the law in the sight of God, it is evident: for, The just shall live by faith.

*Hebrews 10:38 Now the just shall live by faith: but if any man draw back, my soul shall have no pleasure in him.

*John 8:12 Then spake Jesus again unto them, saying, I am the light of the world: he that followeth me shall not walk in darkness, but shall have the light of life.

*Ephesians 5:8 For ye were sometimes darkness, but now are ye light in the Lord: walk as children of light:

*1 John 1:7 But if we walk in the light, as he is in the light, we have fellowship one with another, and the blood of Jesus Christ his Son cleanseth us from all sin.

Authority & Power

Those who know Christ are called of God to walk in a place of authority and power. These I share with you are powerful Scriptures that we need to meditate upon on a daily basis in order to step into this reality. I have included a combination of old and new Testaments Scriptures that will help you to begin to realize this amazing place where Christ has call us to walk and move.

*Daniel 11:32 ..... but the people that do know their God shall be strong, and do exploits.

*Jeremiah 33:3 call unto me, and I will answer thee, and shew thee great and mighty things, which thou knowest not.

*Isaiah 65:24 And it shall come to pass, that before they call, I will answer; and while they are yet speaking, I will hear.

*Ephesians 3:20 Now unto him that is able to do exceeding abundantly above all that we ask or think, according to the power that worketh in us,

*Isaiah 55:6 Seek ye the Lord while he may be found, call ye upon him while he is near:7 Let the wicked forsake his way, and the unrighteous man his thoughts: and let him return unto the Lord, and he will have mercy upon him; and to our God, for he will abundantly pardon.

*Isaiah 45:3 And I will give thee the treasures of darkness, and hidden riches of secret places, that thou mayest know that I, the Lord, which call thee by thy name, am the God of Israel.

*Psalm 25:14 The secret of the Lord is with them that fear him; and he will shew them his covenant.

---

*1 Peter 4:11 If any man speak, let him speak as the oracles of God; if any man minister, let him do it as of the ability which God giveth: that God in all things may be glorified through Jesus Christ, to whom be praise and dominion for ever and ever. Amen.

---

*Acts 1:8 But ye shall receive power, after that the Holy Ghost is come upon you: and ye shall be witnesses unto me both in Jerusalem, and in all Judæa, and in Samaria, and unto the uttermost part of the earth.

---

*Proverbs 28:1 The wicked flee when no man pursueth: but the righteous are bold as a lion.

---

*2 Samuel 23:2 The Spirit of the Lord spake by me, and his word was in my tongue.

---

*Acts 10:38 how God anointed Jesus of Nazareth with the Holy Ghost and with power: who went about doing good, and healing all that were oppressed of the devil; for God was with him.

---

*Matthew 10:8 Heal the sick, cleanse the lepers, raise the dead, cast out devils: freely ye have received, freely give.

---

*Luke 4:18 The Spirit of the Lord is upon me, because he hath anointed me to preach the gospel to the poor; he hath sent me to heal the brokenhearted, to preach deliverance to the captives, and recovering of sight to the blind, to set at liberty them that are bruised, 19 to preach the acceptable year of the Lord.

---

*Numbers 23:19 God is not a man, that he should lie; neither the son of man, that he should repent: hath he said, and shall he not do it? or hath he spoken, and shall he not make it good?

---

*Acts 6:8 And Stephen, full of faith and power, did great wonders and miracles among the people.

---

*Acts 2:17 And it shall come to pass in the last days, saith God, I will pour out of my Spirit upon all flesh: and your sons and your daughters shall prophesy, and your young men shall see visions, and your old men shall dream dreams:18 And on my servants and on my handmaidens I will pour out in those days of my Spirit; and they shall prophesy:

*Luke 10:19 Behold, I give unto you power to tread on serpents and scorpions, and over all the power of the enemy: and nothing shall by any means hurt you.

*2 Samuel 22:35 He teacheth my hands to war; so that a bow of steel is broken by mine arms.

*Matthew 8:9 For I am a man under authority, having soldiers under me: and I say to this man, Go, and he goeth; and to another, Come, and he cometh; and to my servant, Do this, and he doeth it.

*Mark 1:27 And they were all amazed, insomuch that they questioned among themselves, saying, What thing is this? what new doctrine is this? for with authority commandeth he even the unclean spirits, and they do obey him.

*Luke 9:1 Then he called his twelve disciples together, and gave them power and authority over all devils, and to cure diseases.

Complete Agreement

God is diligently searching for those who will simply be in agreement with him. what happened is that when man partook of sin he was put out of harmony with God. Jesus Christ was one with the Father, in word, deed and action. He boldly declared that if you hear me you hear the Father . The words he spoke he declared were not his but the Fathers. Even the works that he did were not of him but from the Father. The last words we hear Christ pray before he went to the garden of Gethsemane were: *Father make them one with us even as we are one!*

*John 17:21 that they all may be one; as thou, Father, art in me, and I in thee, that they also may be one in us: that the world may believe that thou hast sent me. 22 And the glory which thou gavest me I have given them; that they may be one, even as we are one:

*2 Chronicles 16:9 For the eyes of the Lord run to and fro throughout the whole earth, to shew himself strong in the behalf of them whose heart is perfect toward him.

*1 Peter 3:12 For the eyes of the Lord are over the righteous, and his ears are open unto their prayers: but the face of the Lord is against them that do evil.

*Amos 3:3 Can two walk together, except they be agreed?

*Colossians 3:17 - And whatsoever ye do in word or deed, [do] all in the name of the Lord Jesus, giving thanks to God and the Father by him.

Divine Guidance

   Being led by the spirit of God is one of the most important aspects of a believer's life. I cannot tell you how many times my life has been spared because I heard the voice of God. Jesus is very emphatic when he declares that my sheep hear my voice, and another they will not follow. It is extremely important that we become very sensitive to what God is saying to us 1st of all through his word. I actually have written a book about the 20 ways in which God leads and guides his people. Of course one of the major ways that God speaks to us is through his word. As you hide the Scriptures in your heart, meditating upon them, they will become alive on the inside of you . The Holy Spirit will use them to lead and guide you in the exact direction that you need to hear from the heavenly father.

   *Psalms 32:8 - I will instruct thee and teach thee in the way which thou shalt go: I will guide thee with mine eye.

*John 16:13 - Howbeit when he, the Spirit of truth, is come, he will guide you into all truth: for he shall not speak of himself; but whatsoever he shall hear, [that] shall he speak: and he will shew you things to come.

---

*Proverbs 3:5-6 - Trust in the LORD with all thine heart; and lean not unto thine own understanding. 6 In all thy ways acknowledge him, and he shall direct thy paths.

---

*Psalms 119:105 Thy word [is] a lamp unto my feet, and a light unto my path.

---

*Psalm 18:28 For thou wilt light my candle: the Lord my God will enlighten my darkness.

---

*Amos 3:7 Surely the Lord God will do nothing, but he revealeth his secret unto his servants the prophets.

---

*John 15:15 Henceforth I call you not servants; for the servant knoweth not what his lord doeth: but I have called you friends; for all things that I have heard of my Father I have made known unto you.

---

*Psalm 25:14 The secret of the Lord is with them that fear him; and he will shew them his covenant.

---

*Jeremiah 23:22 But if they had stood in my counsel, and had caused my people to hear my words, then they should have turned them from their evil way, and from the evil of their doings.

---

*1 Corinthians 14:24 But if all prophesy, and there come in one that believeth not, or one unlearned, he is convinced of all, he is judged of all: 25 and thus are the secrets of his heart made manifest; and so falling down on his face he will worship God, and report that God is in you of a truth.

---

*John 14:26 - But the Comforter, [which is] the Holy Ghost, whom the Father will send in my name, he shall teach you all things, and bring all things to your remembrance, whatsoever I have said unto you.

---

*James 1:5-6 - If any of you lack wisdom, let him ask of God, that giveth to all [men] liberally, and upbraideth not; and it shall be given him.

*Psalms 37:23-24 - The steps of a [good] man are ordered by the LORD: and he delighteth in his way.

*Psalms 25:9-10 - The meek will he guide in judgment: and the meek will he teach his way.

*2 Timothy 3:16 - All scripture [is] given by inspiration of God, and [is] profitable for doctrine, for reproof, for correction, for instruction in righteousness:

*Isaiah 30:21 - And thine ears shall hear a word behind thee, saying, This [is] the way, walk ye in it, when ye turn to the right hand, and when ye turn to the left.

*Psalms 25:4-5 - Shew me thy ways, O LORD; teach me thy paths.

*1 Peter 4:11 - If any man speak, [let him speak] as the oracles of God; if any man minister, [let him do it] as of the ability which God giveth: that God in all things may be glorified through Jesus Christ, to whom be praise and dominion for ever and ever. Amen.

*Psalms 37:23 - The steps of a [good] man are ordered by the LORD: and he delighteth in his way.

*Psalms 25:5-9 - Lead me in thy truth, and teach me: for thou [art] the God of my salvation; on thee do I wait all the day.

*1 Corinthians 1:30 - But of him are ye in Christ Jesus, who of God is made unto us wisdom, and righteousness, and sanctification, and redemption:

*Psalms 25:12-15 - What man [is] he that feareth the LORD? him shall he teach in the way [that] he shall choose.

*Job 33:14-15 - For God speaketh once, yea twice, [yet man] perceiveth it not.

---

*Isaiah 11:2 - And the spirit of the LORD shall rest upon him, the spirit of wisdom and understanding, the spirit of counsel and might, the spirit of knowledge and of the fear of the LORD;

---

*Psalm 73:24 Thou shalt guide me with thy counsel, and afterward receive me to glory.

---

*Isaiah 58:11 and the Lord shall guide thee continually, and satisfy thy soul in drought, and make fat thy bones: and thou shalt be like a watered garden, and like a spring of water, whose waters fail not.

---

*Luke 1:78 through the tender mercy of our God;whereby the dayspring from on high hath visited us,79 to give light to them that sit in darkness and in the shadow of death,to guide our feet into the way of peace.

---

*Proverbs 6:21 bind them continually upon thine heart,and tie them about thy neck.22 When thou goest, it shall lead thee;when thou sleepest, it shall keep thee;and when thou awakest, it shall talk with thee.23 For the commandment is a lamp; and the law is light;and reproofs of instruction are the way of life:

---

*Isaiah 42:16 And I will bring the blind by a way that they knew not; I will lead them in paths that they have not known: I will make darkness light before them, and crooked things straight. These things will I do unto them, and not forsake them.

---

*Matthew 6:13 And lead us not into temptation, but deliver us from evil: For thine is the kingdom, and the power, and the glory, for ever. Amen.

---

*Revelation 7:17 For the Lamb which is in the midst of the throne shall feed them, and shall lead them unto living fountains of waters: and God shall wipe away all tears from their eyes.

---

*Proverbs 3:5 Trust in the Lord with all thine heart; and lean not unto thine own understanding.6 In all thy ways acknowledge him, and he shall direct thy paths.

---

*Jeremiah 10:23 O Lord, I know that the way of man is not in himself: it is not in man that walketh to direct his steps.

---

*2 Peter 1:21 For the prophecy came not in old time by the will of man: but holy men of God spake as they were moved by the Holy Ghost.

---

*Romans 8:14 For as many as are led by the Spirit of God, they are the sons of God.

---

*Romans 8:5 For they that are after the flesh do mind the things of the flesh; but they that are after the Spirit the things of the Spirit.

---

*Psalm 143:10 Teach me to do thy will; for thou art my God: thy spirit is good; lead me into the land of uprightness.

---

*Proverbs 8:20 I lead in the way of righteousness, in the midst of the paths of judgment:

---

*Proverbs 20:27 The spirit of man is the candle of the Lord, searching all the inward parts of the belly.

---

*Psalm 16:11 Thou wilt shew me the path of life: in thy presence is fulness of joy; at thy right hand there are pleasures for evermore.

We Must Overcome

*Romans 12:21 Be not overcome of evil, but overcome evil with good.

---

*Revelation 3:21 - To him that overcometh will I grant to sit with me in my throne, even as I also overcame, and am set down with my Father in his throne.

*1 John 5:1-21 - Whosoever believeth that Jesus is the Christ is born of God: and every one that loveth him that begat loveth him also that is begotten of him.

*Matthew 7:21-23 - Not every one that saith unto me, Lord, Lord, shall enter into the kingdom of heaven; but he that doeth the will of my Father which is in heaven.

*1 John 5:3 - For this is the love of God, that we keep his commandments: and his commandments are not grievous.

*Hebrews 4:16 - Let us therefore come boldly unto the throne of grace, that we may obtain mercy, and find grace to help in time of need.

*John 12:31 - Now is the judgment of this world: now shall the prince of this world be cast out.

*Jeremiah 17:9 - The heart [is] deceitful above all [things], and desperately wicked: who can know it?

*Isaiah 55:7 - Let the wicked forsake his way, and the unrighteous man his thoughts: and let him return unto the LORD, and he will have mercy upon him; and to our God, for he will abundantly pardon.

*Revelation 2:26 - And he that overcometh, and keepeth my works unto the end, to him will I give power over the nations:

CHAPTER NINE

Defensive Weapons

The Definition of defense is the act or action of defending, or protecting yourself. It is the capability of resisting attack. It is a means or method of defending or protecting oneself, one's team, or another; also : a defensive structure. It could also be a **Truth** in support or justification. In court it is the collected facts and legal methods used by a defendant to protect and defend against a plaintiff's action. In the military there are Weapons specifically used to overcome an attacking enemy!

*James 4:7 Submit yourselves therefore to God. Resist the devil, and he will flee from you.

---

*Acts 6:10 And they were not able to resist the wisdom and the spirit by which he spake.

---

*Hebrews 12:3 For consider him that endured such contradiction of sinners against himself, lest ye be wearied and faint in your minds.4 Ye have not yet resisted unto blood, striving against sin.

---

*1 Corinthians 10:13 There hath no temptation taken you but such as is common to man: but God is faithful, who will not suffer you to be tempted above that ye are able; but will with the temptation also make a way to escape, that ye may be able to bear it.

---

*Matthew 26:41 Watch and pray, that ye enter not into temptation: the spirit indeed is willing, but the flesh is weak.

---

*James 1:12 Blessed is the man that endureth temptation: for when he is tried, he shall receive the crown of life, which the Lord hath promised to them that love him.

---

*2 Peter 2:9 The Lord knoweth how to deliver the godly out of temptations, and to reserve the unjust unto the day of judgment to be punished:

*1 Peter 5:8 Be sober, be vigilant; because your adversary the devil, as a roaring lion, walketh about, seeking whom he may devour:9 Whom resist stedfast in the faith, knowing that the same afflictions are accomplished in your brethren that are in the world.

*Ephesians 4:27 Neither give place to the devil.

*Ephesians 5:21 Submitting yourselves one to another in the fear of God.

*Psalm 66:3 Say unto God, How terrible art thou in thy works! through the greatness of thy power shall thine enemies submit themselves unto thee.

*Psalm 32:5 I acknowledge my sin unto thee, and mine iniquity have I not hid. I said, I will confess my transgressions unto the Lord; and thou forgavest the iniquity of my sin. Selah.

Divine Healing

Healing is such an important part of God's redemptive plan for man. There's many Scriptures that are given to us in the old and the new pertaining to this important subject. As you hide the word of God in your heart through memorization, and meditation may the Scriptures become alive inside of you. May the Lord grant unto you a revelation of the price that was paid for your physical, mental, and emotional healing. For over 40 years I have fought the fight of faith when it comes to divine healing for myself and many others. Christ has paid the ultimate price for my physical healing, and I will not allow the enemy to rob me of it. I hope you will be of the same mindset.

*Isa 53:4-5 Surely he hath borne our griefs, and carried our sorrows: yet we did esteem him stricken, smitten of God, and afflicted....But he was wounded for our transgressions, he was bruised for our iniquities: the chastisement of our peace was upon him; and with his stripes we are healed.

*Prov 4:20-22 My son, attend to my words; incline thine ear unto my sayings….Let them not depart from thine eyes; keep them in the midst of thine heart….For they are life unto those that find them, and health to all their flesh.

---

*3 John 1:2 Beloved, I wish above all things that thou mayest prosper and be in health, even as thy soul prospereth.

---

*1 John 5:14-15 And this is the confidence that we have in him, that, if we ask any thing according to his will, he heareth us:…And if we know that he hear us, whatsoever we ask, we know that we have the petitions that we desired of him.

---

*Isa 41:10 Fear thou not; for I am with thee: be not dismayed; for I am thy God: I will strengthen thee; yea, I will help thee; yea, I will uphold thee with the right hand of my righteousness.

---

*Deut 7:15 And the LORD will take away from thee all sickness, and will put none of the evil diseases of Egypt, which thou knowest, upon thee; but will lay them upon all them that hate thee.

---

*Exo 15:26 And said, If thou wilt diligently hearken to the voice of the LORD thy God, and wilt do that which is right in his sight, and wilt give ear to his commandments, and keep all his statutes, I will put none of these diseases upon thee, which I have brought upon the Egyptians: for I am the LORD that healeth thee.

---

*Jer 30:17 For I will restore health unto thee, and I will heal thee of thy wounds, saith the LORD;

---

*Jer 33:6 Behold, I will bring it health and cure, and I will cure them, and will reveal unto them the abundance of peace and truth.

---

*Isa 58:8 Then shall thy light break forth as the morning, and thine health shall spring forth speedily: and thy righteousness shall go before thee; the glory of the LORD shall be thy rereward.

---

*2 Chr 30:20 And the LORD hearkened to Hezekiah, and healed the people.

*Num 23:19 God is not a man, that he should lie; neither the son of man, that he should repent: hath he said, and shall he not do it? or hath he spoken, and shall he not make it good?

*Psa 105:37 He brought them forth also with silver and gold: and there was not one feeble person among their tribes.

*Psa 103:3 Who forgiveth all thine iniquities; who healeth all thy diseases;

*Psa 147:3 He healeth the broken in heart, and bindeth up their wounds.

*Psa 30:2 O LORD my God, I cried unto thee, and thou hast healed me.

*Psa 34:19 Many are the afflictions of the righteous: but the LORD delivereth him out of them all.

*Psa 42:11 Why art thou cast down, O my soul? and why art thou disquieted within me? hope thou in God: for I shall yet praise him, who is the health of my countenance, and my God.

*Mat 8:17 That it might be fulfilled which was spoken by Esaias the prophet, saying, Himself took our infirmities, and bare our sicknesses.

*1 Pet 2:24 Who his own self bare our sins in his own body on the tree, that we, being dead to sins, should live unto righteousness: by whose stripes ye were healed.

*Gal 3:13,14, Christ hath redeemed us from the curse of the law, being made a curse for us: for it is written, Cursed is every one that hangeth on a tree:…

*Prov 3:1-2 My son, forget not my law; but let thine heart keep my commandments:…For length of days, and long life, and peace, shall they add to thee.

*Mat 4:23-24 And Jesus went about all Galilee, teaching in their synagogues, and preaching the gospel of the kingdom, and healing all manner of sickness and all manner of disease among the people....And his fame went throughout all Syria: and they brought unto him all sick people that were taken with divers diseases and torments, and those which were possessed with devils, and those which were lunatic, and those that had the palsy; and he healed them.

*Mat 12:15 But when Jesus knew it, he withdrew himself from thence: and great multitudes followed him, and he healed them all;

*John 10:10 The thief cometh not, but for to steal, and to kill, and to destroy: I am come that they might have life, and that they might have it more abundantly.

*Acts 10:38 How God anointed Jesus of Nazareth with the Holy Ghost and with power: who went about doing good, and healing all that were oppressed of the devil; for God was with him.

*1 John 3:8 He that committeth sin is of the devil; for the devil sinneth from the beginning. For this purpose the Son of God was manifested, that he might destroy the works of the devil.

*Mat 10:1 And when he had called unto him his twelve disciples, he gave them power against unclean spirits, to cast them out, and to heal all manner of sickness and all manner of disease.

*John 14:12-15 Verily, verily, I say unto you, He that believeth on me, the works that I do shall he do also; and greater works than these shall he do; because I go unto my Father....And whatsoever ye shall ask in my name, that will I do, that the Father may be glorified in the Son....If ye shall ask any thing in my name, I will do it....If ye love me, keep my commandments.

*James 5:14-16 Is any sick among you? let him call for the elders of the church; and let them pray over him, anointing him with oil in the name of the Lord:...And the prayer of faith shall save the sick, and the Lord shall raise him up; and if he have committed sins, they shall be forgiven him....Confess your faults one to another, and pray one for another, that ye may be healed. The effectual fervent prayer of a righteous man availeth much.

*Mal 4:2 But unto you that fear my name shall the Sun of righteousness arise with healing in his wings; and ye shall go forth, and grow up as calves of the stall.

*Psa 107:20 He sent his word, and healed them, and delivered them from their destructions.

*Isa 55:11 So shall my word be that goeth forth out of my mouth: it shall not return unto me void, but it shall accomplish that which I please, and it shall prosper in the thing whereto I sent it.

*Luke 4: 18 The Spirit of the Lord is upon me, because he hath anointed me to preach the gospel to the poor; he hath sent me to heal the brokenhearted, to preach deliverance to the captives, and recovering of sight to the blind, to set at liberty them that are bruised, 19 to preach the acceptable year of the Lord.

Divine Protection

*Psalm 34:19 Many are the afflictions of the righteous: but the Lord delivereth him out of them all.

*Isaiah 54:17 - No weapon that is formed against thee shall prosper; and every tongue [that] shall rise against thee in judgment thou shalt condemn. This [is] the heritage of the servants of the LORD, and their righteousness [is] of me, saith the LORD.

*2 Samuel 22:3 the God of my rock; in him will I trust: he is my shield, and the horn of my salvation, my high tower, and my refuge, my saviour; thou savest me from violence.

*Psalms 91:1 He that dwelleth in the secret place of the most High shall abide under the shadow of the Almighty.

*Psalm 4:8 I will both lay me down in peace, and sleep: for thou, Lord, only makest me dwell in safety.

*Jude 1:24-25 - Now unto him that is able to keep you from falling, and to present [you] faultless before the presence of his glory with exceeding joy,

*Psalm 62:2 He only is my rock and my salvation; he is my defence; I shall not be greatly moved.

*Isaiah 26:3-4 - Thou wilt keep [him] in perfect peace, [whose] mind [is] stayed [on thee]: because he trusteth in thee.

*Psalm 91:4 He shall cover thee with his feathers, and under his wings shalt thou trust: his truth shall be thy shield and buckler.

*1 Peter 2:9 - But ye [are] a chosen generation, a royal priesthood, an holy nation, a peculiar people; that ye should shew forth the praises of him who hath called you out of darkness into his marvellous light:

*John 10:10 - The thief cometh not, but for to steal, and to kill, and to destroy: I am come that they might have life, and that they might have [it] more abundantly.

*John 8:32 - And ye shall know the truth, and the truth shall make you free.

*Psalms 121:1 I will lift up mine eyes unto the hills, from whence cometh my help.

*Psalms 46:1 God [is] our refuge and strength, a very present help in trouble.

*Hebrews 4:16 - Let us therefore come boldly unto the throne of grace, that we may obtain mercy, and find grace to help in time of need.

*1 John 3:8 ..... For this purpose the Son of God was manifested, that he might destroy the works of the devil.

*Philippians 4:19 - But my God shall supply all your need according to his riches in glory by Christ Jesus.

*Ephesians 1:3 - Blessed [be] the God and Father of our Lord Jesus Christ, who hath blessed us with all spiritual blessings in heavenly [places] in Christ:

*Isaiah 43:2 When thou passest through the waters, I will be with thee; and through the rivers, they shall not overflow thee: when thou walkest through the fire, thou shalt not be burned; neither shall the flame kindle upon thee.

Praise, Worship, Thanksgiving,

*Philippians 4:6 - Be careful for nothing; but in everything by prayer and supplication with thanksgiving let your requests be made known unto God.

*Psalms 7:17 - I will praise the LORD according to his righteousness: and will sing praise to the name of the LORD most high.

*1 Thessalonians 5:18 - In everything give thanks: for this is the will of God in Christ Jesus concerning you.

*Psalms 107:1 - O give thanks unto the LORD, for [he is] good: for his mercy [endureth] forever.

*Ephesians 5:20 - Giving thanks always for all things unto God and the Father in the name of our Lord Jesus Christ;

*Psalms 50:14 - Offer unto God thanksgiving; and pay thy vows unto the most High:

*Psalms 100:1 Make a joyful noise unto the LORD, all ye lands.

*Hebrews 13:15 - By him therefore let us offer the sacrifice of praise to God continually, that is, the fruit of [our] lips giving thanks to his name.

*Luke 6:38 - Give, and it shall be given unto you; good measure, pressed down, and shaken together, and running over, shall men give into your bosom. For with the same measure that ye *Colossians 3:15 - And let the peace of God rule in your hearts, to the which also ye are called in one body; and be ye thankful.

*Habakkuk 3:17 - Although the fig tree shall not blossom, neither [shall] fruit [be] in the vines; the labour of the olive shall fail, and the fields shall yield no meat; the flock shall be cut off from the fold, and [there shall be] no herd in the stalls:

*Psalms 92:1 [It is a] good [thing] to give thanks unto the LORD, and to sing praises unto thy name, O most High:

*1 Thessalonians 5:17 - Pray without ceasing.

*Psalms 95:6 - O come, let us worship and bow down: let us kneel before the LORD our maker.

*Matthew 18:20 - For where two or three are gathered together in my name, there am I in the midst of them.

*John 4:23 - But the hour cometh, and now is, when the true worshippers shall worship the Father in spirit and in truth: for the Father seeketh such to worship him.

*Psalms 29:2 - Give unto the LORD the glory due unto his name; worship the LORD in the beauty of holiness.

*1 Peter 2:5 - Ye also, as lively stones, are built up a spiritual house, an holy priesthood, to offer up spiritual sacrifices, acceptable to God by Jesus Christ.

*Psalms 96:9 - O worship the LORD in the beauty of holiness: fear before him, all the earth.

*Psalms 95:1-6 - O come, let us sing unto the LORD: let us make a joyful noise to the rock of our salvation.

*Psalms 96:8 - Give unto the LORD the glory [due unto] his name: bring an offering, and come into his courts.

*Acts 16:25 – And at midnight Paul and Silas prayed, and sang praises unto God: and the prisoners heard them.

Divine Provisions

*Deuteronomy 8:18 But thou shalt remember the Lord thy God: for it is he that giveth thee power to get wealth, that he may establish his covenant which he sware unto thy fathers, as it is this day.

*Hebrews 13:5 - [Let your] conversation [be] without covetousness; [and be] content with such things as ye have: for he hath said, I will never leave thee, nor forsake thee.

*2 Peter 1:3 - According as his divine power hath given unto us all things that [pertain] unto life and godliness, through the knowledge of him that hath called us to glory and virtue:

*2 Corinthians 1:20 For all the promises of God in him are yea, and in him Amen, unto the glory of God by us.

Psalm 112:3 Wealth and riches shall be in his house: and his righteousness endureth forever.

Ecclesiastes 5:19 Every man also to whom God hath given riches and wealth, and hath given him power to eat thereof, and to take his portion, and to rejoice in his labour; this is the gift of God.

Malachi 3:10 - Bring ye all the tithes into the storehouse, that there may be meat in mine house, and prove me now herewith, saith the LORD of hosts, if I will not open you the windows of heaven, and pour you out a blessing, that [there shall] not [be room] enough [to receive it].

2 Corinthians 9:8 - And God [is] able to make all grace abound toward you; that ye, always having all sufficiency in all [things], may abound to every good work:

Psalms 1:3 - And he shall be like a tree planted by the rivers of water, that bringeth forth his fruit in his season; his leaf also shall not wither; and whatsoever he doeth shall prosper.

2 Corinthians 8:9 - For ye know the grace of our Lord Jesus Christ, that, though he was rich, yet for your sakes he became poor, that ye through his poverty might be rich.

Job 22:23-27 - If thou return to the Almighty, thou shalt be built up, thou shalt put away iniquity far from thy tabernacles.

Proverbs 28:25 - He that is of a proud heart stirreth up strife: but he that putteth his trust in the LORD shall be made fat.

Zechariah 9:12 - Turn you to the strong hold, ye prisoners of hope: even to day do I declare [that] I will render double unto thee;

Nehemiah 2:20 - ....The God of heaven, he will prosper us; therefore we his servants will arise and build: but ye have no portion, nor right, nor memorial, in Jerusalem.

Jeremiah 29:11-14 - For I know the thoughts that I think toward you, saith the LORD, thoughts of peace, and not of evil, to give you an expected end. (Read More...)

Psalms 1:1-6 - Blessed [is] the man that walketh not in the counsel of the ungodly, nor standeth in the way of sinners, nor sitteth in the seat of the scornful. (Read More...)

Jeremiah 17:10 - I the LORD search the heart, [I] try the reins, even to give every man according to his ways, [and] according to the fruit of his doings.

Deuteronomy 28:1-14 - And it shall come to pass, if thou shalt hearken diligently unto the voice of the LORD thy God, to observe [and] to do all his commandments which I command thee this day, that the LORD thy God will set thee on high above all nations of the earth: (Read More...)

Luke 6:38 - Give, and it shall be given unto you; good measure, pressed down, and shaken together, and running over, shall men give into your bosom. For with the same measure that ye mete withal it shall be measured to you again.

God's Grace

Grace is one of the most misunderstood subjects of the Bible. They have confused it with the subject of God's mercy. Grace is a Greek word by which we get the word charisma. It means the divine ability of God at work in a believer. Paul says that by the grace of God I am what I am. He also tells us that the grace of God should not be in vain in regards to overcoming sin. Calvinism seems to have penetrated every part of the modern day church (once saved, always saved). So many are being deceived by the sloppy agape, greasy grace I'm okay you're okay message.

Christ did not come to leave us in our sin, defeated by the devil and immorality. He came to give us a new nature with victory over sin. It's amazing how many people are being deceived by this false doctrine. In the book of Revelation, JESUS never talks about grace, but he does goes on and on about works. Jesus said in the book of Revelation chapter 1 to chapter 3, I know thy works. I think people are willingly ignorant of the importance of the works that is produced in us, because of Christ Jesus, and our faith in him, that produces obedience. no matter how many scriptures you present to people in contexts, they will still disagree with the fact that right after chapter 2 in Ephesians were it says that we are saved by grace, it goes on to say that we are created unto good works. No it is not me doing the good works, but it is Christ doing them in me, and through me.

*2 Corinthians 12:9 - And he said unto me, My grace is sufficient for thee: for my strength is made perfect in weakness. Most gladly therefore will I rather glory in my infirmities, that the power of Christ may rest upon me.

*Ephesians 2:5 Even when we were dead in sins, hath quickened us together with Christ, (by grace ye are saved;):8 For by grace are ye saved through faith; and that not of yourselves: it is the gift of God:

*Romans 6:14 - For sin shall not have dominion over you: for ye are not under the law, but under grace.

*Romans 11:6 - And if by grace, then [is it] no more of works: otherwise grace is no more grace. But if [it be] of works, then is it no more grace: otherwise work is no more work.

*James 4:6 - But he giveth more grace. Wherefore he saith, God resisteth the proud, but giveth grace unto the humble.

*1 Corinthians 15:10 - But by the grace of God I am what I am: and his grace which [was bestowed] upon me was not in vain; but I laboured more abundantly than they all: yet not I, but the grace of God which was with me.

*Romans 5:8 - But God commendeth his love toward us, in that, while we were yet sinners, Christ died for us.

*Hebrews 4:16 - Let us therefore come boldly unto the throne of grace, that we may obtain mercy, and find grace to help in time of need.

*John 1:16 - And of his fulness have all we received, and grace for grace. 17 For the law was given by Moses, but grace and truth came by Jesus Christ.

*Romans 3:24 - Being justified freely by his grace through the redemption that is in Christ Jesus:

*2 Timothy 2:1 - Thou therefore, my son, be strong in the grace that is in Christ Jesus.

*2 Timothy 4:22 - The Lord Jesus Christ [be] with thy spirit. Grace [be] with you. Amen.

---

*Isaiah 40:31 - But they that wait upon the LORD shall renew [their] strength; they shall mount up with wings as eagles; they shall run, and not be weary; [and] they shall walk, and not faint.

---

*Romans 1:5 By whom we have received grace and apostleship, for obedience to the faith among all nations, for his name:

---

*Romans 4:16 Therefore it is of faith, that it might be by grace; to the end the promise might be sure to all the seed; not to that only which is of the law, but to that also which is of the faith of Abraham; who is the father of us all,

---

*Romans 5:21 That as sin hath reigned unto death, even so might grace reign through righteousness unto eternal life by Jesus Christ our Lord.

---

1 Corinthians 15:10 But by the grace of God I am what I am: and his grace which was bestowed upon me was not in vain; but I laboured more abundantly than they all: yet not I, but the grace of God which was with me.

CHAPTER TEN

Adversity

2 Corinthians 4:8-9 - [We are] troubled on every side, yet not distressed; [we are] perplexed, but not in despair;

Philippians 4:12-13 - I know both how to be abased, and I know how to abound: everywhere and in all things I am instructed both to be full and to be hungry, both to abound and to suffer need.

Proverbs 24:10 - [If] thou faint in the day of adversity, thy strength [is] small.

---

1 Peter 5:10 - But the God of all grace, who hath called us unto his eternal glory by Christ Jesus, after that ye have suffered a while, make you perfect, stablish, strengthen, settle [you].

---

2 Corinthians 12:9 - And he said unto me, My grace is sufficient for thee: for my strength is made perfect in weakness. Most gladly therefore will I rather glory in my infirmities, that the power of Christ may rest upon me.

Romans 8:28 - And we know that all things work together for good to them that love God, to them who are the called according to [his] purpose.

Joshua 1:9 - Have not I commanded thee? Be strong and of a good courage; be not afraid, neither be thou dismayed: for the LORD thy God [is] with thee whithersoever thou goest.

---

2 Chronicles 15:7 - Be ye strong therefore, and let not your hands be weak: for your work shall be rewarded.

Romans 12:2 - And be not conformed to this world: but be ye transformed by the renewing of your mind, that ye may prove what [is] that good, and acceptable, and perfect, will of God.

Revelation 21:4 - And God shall wipe away all tears from their eyes; and there shall be no more death, neither sorrow, nor crying, neither shall there be any more pain: for the former things are passed away.

Psalms 34:19 - Many [are] the afflictions of the righteous: but the LORD delivereth him out of them all.

1 Peter 4:12-13 - Beloved, think it not strange concerning the fiery trial which is to try you, as though some strange thing happened unto you:

2 Corinthians 1:4 - Who comforteth us in all our tribulation, that we may be able to comfort them which are in any trouble, by the comfort wherewith we ourselves are comforted of God.

Anger

James 1:19 - Wherefore, my beloved brethren, let every man be swift to hear, slow to speak, slow to wrath:

Ecclesiastes 7:9 - Be not hasty in thy spirit to be angry: for anger resteth in the bosom of fools.

John 14:27 - Peace I leave with you, my peace I give unto you: not as the world giveth, give I unto you. Let not your heart be troubled, neither let it be afraid.

Ephesians 4:26 - Be ye angry, and sin not: let not the sun go down upon your wrath:

Proverbs 16:32 - [He that is] slow to anger [is] better than the mighty; and he that ruleth his spirit than he that taketh a city.

2 Timothy 2:24 - And the servant of the Lord must not strive; but be gentle unto all [men], apt to teach, patient,

Proverbs 22:6 - Train up a child in the way he should go: and when he is old, he will not depart from it.

Ephesians 4:26-27 - Be ye angry, and sin not: let not the sun go down upon your wrath:

Proverbs 25:28 - He that [hath] no rule over his own spirit [is like] a city [that is] broken down, [and] without walls.

Proverbs 29:11 - A fool uttereth all his mind: but a wise [man] keepeth it in till afterwards.

1 Timothy 3:3 - Not given to wine, no striker, not greedy of filthy lucre; but patient, not a brawler, not covetous;

Comfort

2 Corinthians 1:3-4 - Blessed [be] God, even the Father of our Lord Jesus Christ, the Father of mercies, and the God of all comfort;

Romans 8:32-39 - He that spared not his own Son, but delivered him up for us all, how shall he not with him also freely give us all things?

Matthew 11:28-30 - Come unto me, all [ye] that labour and are heavy laden, and I will give you rest.

Isaiah 40:1-2 - Comfort ye, comfort ye my people, saith your God.

Romans 8:26-28 - Likewise the Spirit also helpeth our infirmities: for we know not what we should pray for as we ought: but the Spirit itself maketh intercession for us with groanings which cannot be uttered.

Psalms 91:1-16 - He that dwelleth in the secret place of the most High shall abide under the shadow of the Almighty.

Psalms 23:4 - Yea, though I walk through the valley of the shadow of death, I will fear no evil: for thou [art] with me; thy rod and thy staff they comfort me.

Psalms 86:17 - Shew me a token for good; that they which hate me may see [it], and be ashamed: because thou, LORD, hast holpen me, and comforted me.

Dependability

Luke 16:10 - He that is faithful in that which is least is faithful also in much: and he that is unjust in the least is unjust also in much.

---

2 Timothy 3:16 - All scripture [is] given by inspiration of God, and [is] profitable for doctrine, for reproof, for correction, for instruction in righteousness:

---

1 Corinthians 4:2-4 - Moreover it is required in stewards, that a man be found faithful.   (Read More...)

Hebrews 4:12 - For the word of God [is] quick, and powerful, and sharper than any twoedged sword, piercing even to the dividing asunder of soul and spirit, and of the joints and marrow, and [is] a discerner of the thoughts and intents of the heart.

---

2 Peter 1:20-21 - Knowing this first, that no prophecy of the scripture is of any private interpretation.

Duty

1 Timothy 5:8 - But if any provide not for his own, and specially for those of his own house, he hath denied the faith, and is worse than an infidel.

1 Peter 3:7 - Likewise, ye husbands, dwell with [them] according to knowledge, giving honour unto the wife, as unto the weaker vessel, and as being heirs together of the grace of life; that your prayers be not hindered.

Ephesians 5:25 - Husbands, love your wives, even as Christ also loved the church, and gave himself for it;

1 Timothy 3:4 - One that ruleth well his own house, having his children in subjection with all gravity;

1 Corinthians 16:13 - Watch ye, stand fast in the faith, quit you like men, be strong.

1 Corinthians 15:58 - Therefore, my beloved brethren, be ye stedfast, unmoveable, always abounding in the work of the Lord, forasmuch as ye know that your labour is not in vain in the Lord.

Galatians 3:28 - There is neither Jew nor Greek, there is neither bond nor free, there is neither male nor female: for ye are all one in Christ Jesus.

Genesis 1:26-27 - And God said, Let us make man in our image, after our likeness: and let them have dominion over the fish of the sea, and over the fowl of the air, and over the cattle, and over all the earth, and over every creeping thing that creepeth upon the earth.

Titus 2:3-5 - The aged women likewise, that [they be] in behaviour as becometh holiness, not false accusers, not given to much wine, teachers of good things

Joshua 24:14-15 - Now therefore fear the LORD, and serve him in sincerity and in truth: and put away the gods which your fathers served on the other side of the flood, and in Egypt; and serve ye the LORD.

2 Thessalonians 3:10 - For even when we were with you, this we commanded you, that if any would not work, neither should he eat.

Proverbs 22:6 - Train up a child in the way he should go: and when he is old, he will not depart from it.

Deuteronomy 28:1-68 - And it shall come to pass, if thou shalt hearken diligently unto the voice of the LORD thy God, to observe [and] to do all his commandments which I command thee this day, that the LORD thy God will set thee on high above all nations of the earth.

Encouragement

Joshua 1:9 - Have not I commanded thee? Be strong and of a good courage; be not afraid, neither be thou dismayed: for the LORD thy God [is] with thee whithersoever thou goest.

2 Timothy 1:7 - For God hath not given us the spirit of fear; but of power, and of love, and of a sound mind.

Psalms 121:1-8 - (A Song of degrees.) I will lift up mine eyes unto the hills, from whence cometh my help.

Psalms 37:4 - Delight thyself also in the LORD; and he shall give thee the desires of thine heart.

Proverbs 30:5 - Every word of God [is] pure: he [is] a shield unto them that put their trust in him.

Psalms 28:7 - The LORD [is] my strength and my shield; my heart trusted in him, and I am helped: therefore my heart greatly rejoiceth; and with my song will I praise him.

Psalms 34:4 - I sought the LORD, and he heard me, and delivered me from all my fears.

1 Thessalonians 5:9-11 - For God hath not appointed us to wrath, but to obtain salvation by our Lord Jesus Christ,

Philippians 4:13 - I can do all things through Christ which strengtheneth me.

Psalms 55:22 - Cast thy burden upon the LORD, and he shall sustain thee: he shall never suffer the righteous to be moved.

Romans 15:13 - Now the God of hope fill you with all joy and peace in believing, that ye may abound in hope, through the power of the Holy Ghost.

Jeremiah 29:11 - For I know the thoughts that I think toward you, saith the LORD, thoughts of peace, and not of evil, to give you an expected end.

Psalms 126:5 - They that sow in tears shall reap in joy.

Jeremiah 29:11-14 - For I know the thoughts that I think toward you, saith the LORD, thoughts of peace, and not of evil, to give you an expected end.

Hebrews 10:25 - Not forsaking the assembling of ourselves together, as the manner of some [is]; but exhorting [one another]: and so much the more, as ye see the day approaching.

Ephesians 4:29 - Let no corrupt communication proceed out of your mouth, but that which is good to the use of edifying, that it may minister grace unto the hearers.

Generosity

Acts 20:35 - I have shewed you all things, how that so labouring ye ought to support the weak, and to remember the words of the Lord Jesus, how he said, It is more blessed to give than to receive.

Luke 6:38 - Give, and it shall be given unto you; good measure, pressed down, and shaken together, and running over, shall men give into your bosom. For with the same measure that ye mete withal it shall be measured to you again.

Proverbs 11:24-25 - There is that scattereth, and yet increaseth; and [there is] that withholdeth more than is meet, but [it tendeth] to poverty.

Matthew 6:21 - For where your treasure is, there will your heart be also.

Matthew 10:42 - And whosoever shall give to drink unto one of these little ones a cup of cold [water] only in the name of a disciple, verily I say unto you, he shall in no wise lose his reward.

---

1 John 3:17 - But whoso hath this world's good, and seeth his brother have need, and shutteth up his bowels [of compassion] from him, how dwelleth the love of God in him?

---

1 Timothy 6:17-19 - Charge them that are rich in this world, that they be not highminded, nor trust in uncertain riches, but in the living God, who giveth us richly all things to enjoy;

---

2 Corinthians 9:6 - But this [I say], He which soweth sparingly shall reap also sparingly; and he which soweth bountifully shall reap also bountifully.

Proverbs 19:17 - He that hath pity upon the poor lendeth unto the LORD; and that which he hath given will he pay him again.

Proverbs 21:13 - Whoso stoppeth his ears at the cry of the poor, he also shall cry himself, but shall not be heard.

Luke 12:33 - Sell that ye have, and give alms; provide yourselves bags which wax not old, a treasure in the heavens that faileth not, where no thief approacheth, neither moth corrupteth.

---

1 Timothy 6:18-19 - That they do good, that they be rich in good works, ready to distribute, willing to communicate;

---

2 Corinthians 9:7 - Every man according as he purposeth in his heart, [so let him give]; not grudgingly, or of necessity: for God loveth a cheerful giver.

Matthew 6:1-4 - Take heed that ye do not your alms before men, to be seen of them: otherwise ye have no reward of your Father which is in heaven.

Gratitude

Psalms 118:24 - This [is] the day [which] the LORD hath made; we will rejoice and be glad in it.

1 Thessalonians 5:18 - In everything give thanks: for this is the will of God in Christ Jesus concerning you.

Colossians 3:17 - And whatsoever ye do in word or deed, [do] all in the name of the Lord Jesus, giving thanks to God and the Father by him.

Psalms 127:1 - (A Song of degrees for Solomon.) Except the LORD build the house, they labour in vain that build it: except the LORD keep the city, the watchman waketh [but] in vain.

Hebrews 12:28 - Wherefore we receiving a kingdom which cannot be moved, let us have grace, whereby we may serve God acceptably with reverence and godly fear:

Colossians 3:15 - And let the peace of God rule in your hearts, to the which also ye are called in one body; and be ye thankful.

Psalms 107:1 - O give thanks unto the LORD, for [he is] good: for his mercy [endureth] for ever.

Psalms 50:23 - Whoso offereth praise glorifieth me: and to him that ordereth [his] conversation [aright] will I shew the salvation of God.

Psalms 100:1-5 - (A Psalm of praise.) Make a joyful noise unto the LORD, all ye lands.

Ephesians 5:20 - Giving thanks always for all things unto God and the Father in the name of our Lord Jesus Christ;

Justice

Proverbs 21:15 - [It is] joy to the just to do judgment: but destruction [shall be] to the workers of iniquity.

Amos 5:24 - But let judgment run down as waters, and righteousness as a mighty stream.

Romans 12:19 - Dearly beloved, avenge not yourselves, but [rather] give place unto wrath: for it is written, Vengeance [is] mine; I will repay, saith the Lord.

Micah 6:8 - He hath shewed thee, O man, what [is] good; and what doth the LORD require of thee, but to do justly, and to love mercy, and to walk humbly with thy God?

Psalms 37:27-29 - Depart from evil, and do good; and dwell for evermore

Isaiah 1:17 - Learn to do well; seek judgment, relieve the oppressed, judge the fatherless, plead for the widow.

Proverbs 24:24-25 - He that saith unto the wicked, Thou [art] righteous; him shall the people curse, nations shall abhor him:

Romans 13:4 - For he is the minister of God to thee for good. But if thou do that which is evil, be afraid; for he beareth not the sword in vain: for he is the minister of God, a revenger to [execute] wrath upon him that doeth evil.

Isaiah 61:8 - For I the LORD love judgment, I hate robbery for burnt offering; and I will direct their work in truth, and I will make an everlasting covenant with them.

Luke 6:37 - Judge not, and ye shall not be judged: condemn not, and ye shall not be condemned: forgive, and ye shall be forgiven:

Psalms 50:6 - And the heavens shall declare his righteousness: for God [is] judge himself. Selah.

Ecclesiastes 3:17 - I said in mine heart, God shall judge the righteous and the wicked: for [there is] a time there for every purpose and for every work.

Zechariah 7:9 - Thus speaketh the LORD of hosts, saying, Execute true judgment, and shew mercy and compassions every man to his brother:

Labor

1 Corinthians 15:58 - Therefore, my beloved brethren, be ye stedfast, unmoveable, always abounding in the work of the Lord, forasmuch as ye know that your labour is not in vain in the Lord.

Acts 20:35 - I have shewed you all things, how that so labouring ye ought to support the weak, and to remember the words of the Lord Jesus, how he said, It is more blessed to give than to receive.

Luke 10:7 - And in the same house remain, eating and drinking such things as they give: for the labourer is worthy of his hire. Go not from house to house.

1 Thessalonians 4:11 - And that ye study to be quiet, and to do your own business, and to work with your own hands, as we commanded you;

Ephesians 4:28 - Let him that stole steal no more: but rather let him labour, working with [his] hands the thing which is good, that he may have to give to him that needeth.

1 Timothy 5:18 - For the scripture saith, Thou shalt not muzzle the ox that treadeth out the corn. And, The labourer [is] worthy of his reward.

Ecclesiastes 5:12 - The sleep of a labouring man [is] sweet, whether he eat little or much: but the abundance of the rich will not suffer him to sleep

Colossians 3:23 - And whatsoever ye do, do [it] heartily, as to the Lord, and not unto men;

2 Thessalonians 3:10 - For even when we were with you, this we commanded you, that if any would not work, neither should he eat.

Proverbs 14:23 - In all labour there is profit: but the talk of the lips [tendeth] only to penury.

Proverbs 16:3 - Commit thy works unto the LORD, and thy thoughts shall be established.

Proverbs 10:4 - He becometh poor that dealeth [with] a slack hand: but the hand of the diligent maketh rich.

Ecclesiastes 9:10 - Whatsoever thy hand findeth to do, do [it] with thy might; for [there is] no work, nor device, nor knowledge, nor wisdom, in the grave, whither thou goest.

Proverbs 12:11 - He that tilleth his land shall be satisfied with bread: but he that followeth vain [persons is] void of understanding.

Proverbs 21:25 - The desire of the slothful killeth him; for his hands refuse to labour.

Proverbs 22:29 - Seest thou a man diligent in his business? he shall stand before kings; he shall not stand before mean [men].

Proverbs 13:4 - The soul of the sluggard desireth, and [hath] nothing: but the soul of the diligent shall be made fat.

Repentance

2 Chronicles 7:14 - If my people, which are called by my name, shall humble themselves, and pray, and seek my face, and turn from their wicked ways; then will I hear from heaven, and will forgive their sin, and will heal their land.

---

1 John 1:9 - If we confess our sins, he is faithful and just to forgive us [our] sins, and to cleanse us from all unrighteousness.

Acts 3:19 - Repent ye therefore, and be converted, that your sins may be blotted out, when the times of refreshing shall come from the presence of the Lord;

Luke 13:3 - I tell you, Nay: but, except ye repent, ye shall all likewise perish.

Ezekiel 18:21-23 - But if the wicked will turn from all his sins that he hath committed, and keep all my statutes, and do that which is lawful and right, he shall surely live, he shall not die.

Acts 17:30 - And the times of this ignorance God winked at; but now commandeth all men everywhere to repent:

---

2 Peter 3:9 - The Lord is not slack concerning his promise, as some men count slackness; but is longsuffering to us-ward, not willing that any should perish, but that all should come to repentance.

Proverbs 28:13 - He that covereth his sins shall not prosper: but whoso confesseth and forsaketh [them] shall have mercy.

James 4:8-10 - Draw nigh to God, and he will draw nigh to you. Cleanse [your] hands, [ye] sinners; and purify [your] hearts, [ye] double minded.

Revelation 2:5 - Remember therefore from whence thou art fallen, and repent, and do the first works; or else I will come unto thee quickly, and will remove thy candlestick out of his place, except thou repent.

Acts 2:38 - Then Peter said unto them, Repent, and be baptized every one of you in the name of Jesus Christ for the remission of sins, and ye shall receive the gift of the Holy Ghost.

Righteousness

1 John 2:29 - If ye know that he is righteous, ye know that every one that doeth righteousness is born of him.

Psalms 106:3 - Blessed [are] they that keep judgment, [and] he that doeth righteousness at all times.

Isaiah 33:15-17 - He that walketh righteously, and speaketh uprightly; he that despiseth the gain of oppressions, that shaketh his hands from holding of bribes, that stoppeth his ears from hearing of blood, and shutteth his eyes from seeing evil;

1 John 3:7 - Little children, let no man deceive you: he that doeth righteousness is righteous, even as he is righteous.

1 Peter 3:14 - But and if ye suffer for righteousness' sake, happy [are ye]: and be not afraid of their terror, neither be troubled;

Matthew 5:20 - For I say unto you, That except your righteousness shall exceed [the righteousness] of the scribes and Pharisees, ye shall in no case enter into the kingdom of heaven.

Philippians 1:11 - Being filled with the fruits of righteousness, which are by Jesus Christ, unto the glory and praise of God.

Proverbs 2:5-20 - Then shalt thou understand the fear of the LORD, and find the knowledge of God.

2 Timothy 2:22 - Flee also youthful lusts: but follow righteousness, faith, charity, peace, with them that call on the Lord out of a pure heart.

Salvation

Mark 16:16 - He that believeth and is baptized shall be saved; but he that believeth not shall be damned.

Acts 2:38 - Then Peter said unto them, Repent, and be baptized every one of you in the name of Jesus Christ for the remission of sins, and ye shall receive the gift of the Holy Ghost.

Romans 10:9 - That if thou shalt confess with thy mouth the Lord Jesus, and shalt believe in thine heart that God hath raised him from the dead, thou shalt be saved.

John 3:16-17 - For God so loved the world, that he gave his only begotten Son, that whosoever believeth in him should not perish, but have everlasting life.

Romans 5:8 - But God commendeth his love toward us, in that, while we were yet sinners, Christ died for us.

Acts 4:12 - Neither is there salvation in any other: for there is none other name under heaven given among men, whereby we must be saved.

Galatians 3:27 - For as many of you as have been baptized into Christ have put on Christ.

Romans 10:8-10 - But what saith it? The word is nigh thee, [even] in thy mouth, and in thy heart: that is, the word of faith, which we preach;

Acts 2:41 - Then they that gladly received his word were baptized: and the same day there were added [unto them] about three thousand souls.

James 2:18 - Yea, a man may say, Thou hast faith, and I have works: shew me thy faith without thy works, and I will shew thee my faith by my works.

Isaiah 55:6-7 - Seek ye the LORD while he may be found, call ye upon him while he is near:

Romans 10:11-13 - For the scripture saith, Whosoever believeth on him shall not be ashamed.

James 2:24 - Ye see then how that by works a man is justified, and not by faith only.

Matthew 7:21 - Not everyone that saith unto me, Lord, Lord, shall enter into the kingdom of heaven; but he that doeth the will of my Father which is in heaven.

John 3:5 - Jesus answered, Verily, verily, I say unto thee, Except a man be born of water and [of] the Spirit, he cannot enter into the kingdom of God.

Luke 8:13 - They on the rock [are they], which, when they hear, receive the word with joy; and these have no root, which for a while believe, and in time of temptation fall away.

Seeking God

Deuteronomy 4:29 - But if from thence thou shalt seek the LORD thy God, thou shalt find [him], if thou seek him with all thy heart and with all thy soul.

Proverbs 8:17 - I love them that love me; and those that seek me early shall find me.

Jeremiah 29:12-14 - Then shall ye call upon me, and ye shall go and pray unto me, and I will hearken unto you.

Matthew 7:7-8 - Ask, and it shall be given you; seek, and ye shall find; knock, and it shall be opened unto you:

1 Chronicles 16:11 - Seek the LORD and his strength, seek his face continually.

Lamentations 3:25 - The LORD [is] good unto them that wait for him, to the soul [that] seeketh him.

Isaiah 55:6-7 - Seek ye the LORD while he may be found, call ye upon him while he is near:

Psalms 119:10 - With my whole heart have I sought thee: O let me not wander from thy commandments.

Jeremiah 29:13 - And ye shall seek me, and find [me], when ye shall search for me with all your heart.

Hebrews 11:6 - But without faith [it is] impossible to please [him]: for he that cometh to God must believe that he is, and [that] he is a rewarder of them that diligently seek him.

Psalms 34:10 - The young lions do lack, and suffer hunger: but they that seek the LORD shall not want any good [thing].

Psalms 40:16 - Let all those that seek thee rejoice and be glad in thee: let such as love thy salvation say continually, The LORD be magnified.

Psalms 63:1 O God, thou [art] my God; early will I seek thee: my soul thirsteth for thee, my flesh longeth for thee in a dry and thirsty land, where no water is;

Psalms 119:2 - Blessed [are] they that keep his testimonies, [and that] seek him with the whole heart.

Psalms 9:10 - And they that know thy name will put their trust in thee: for thou, LORD, hast not forsaken them that seek thee.

Psalms 14:2 - The LORD looked down from heaven upon the children of men, to see if there were any that did understand, [and] seek God.

James 4:8 - Draw nigh to God, and he will draw nigh to you. Cleanse [your] hands, [ye] sinners; and purify [your] hearts, [ye] double minded.

Selfishness

Philippians 2:4 - Look not every man on his own things, but every man also on the things of others.

1 John 3:17 - But whoso hath this world's good, and seeth his brother have need, and shutteth up his bowels [of compassion] from him, how dwelleth the love of God in him?

1 Corinthians 10:24 - Let no man seek his own, but every man another's [wealth].

2 Timothy 3:2-4 - For men shall be lovers of their own selves, covetous, boasters, proud, blasphemers, disobedient to parents, unthankful, unholy,

Philippians 2:3-4 - [Let] nothing [be done] through strife or vainglory; but in lowliness of mind let each esteem other better than themselves.

Philippians 2:21 - For all seek their own, not the things which are Jesus Christ's.

Galatians 6:2 - Bear ye one another's burdens, and so fulfil the law of Christ.

Romans 15:1-3 - We then that are strong ought to bear the infirmities of the weak, and not to please ourselves.

James 4:1-2 - From whence [come] wars and fightings among you? [come they] not hence, [even] of your lusts that war in your members?

Galatians 5:26 - Let us not be desirous of vain glory, provoking one another, envying one another.

1 Timothy 6:17-19 - Charge them that are rich in this world, that they be not highminded, nor trust in uncertain riches, but in the living God, who giveth us richly all things to enjoy;

Proverbs 28:27 - He that giveth unto the poor shall not lack: but he that hideth his eyes shall have many a curse.

Luke 6:32-34 - For if ye love them which love you, what thank have ye? for sinners also love those that love them.

Proverbs 21:13 - Whoso stoppeth his ears at the cry of the poor, he also shall cry himself, but shall not be heard.

Hebrews 13:16 - But to do good and to communicate forget not: for with such sacrifices God is well pleased.

Sin

James 4:17 - Therefore to him that knoweth to do good, and doeth [it] not, to him it is sin.

Romans 6:23 - For the wages of sin [is] death; but the gift of God [is] eternal life through Jesus Christ our Lord.

1 John 1:8-10 - If we say that we have no sin, we deceive ourselves, and the truth is not in us.

Romans 3:23 - For all have sinned, and come short of the glory of God;

1 John 3:4 - Whosoever committeth sin transgresseth also the law: for sin is the transgression of the law.

1 John 5:17 - All unrighteousness is sin: and there is a sin not unto death.

Galatians 5:19-21 - Now the works of the flesh are manifest, which are [these]; Adultery, fornication, uncleanness, lasciviousness,

James 1:15 - Then when lust hath conceived, it bringeth forth sin: and sin, when it is finished, bringeth forth death.

Matthew 5:28 - But I say unto you, That whosoever looketh on a woman to lust after her hath committed adultery with her already in his heart.

2 Corinthians 5:17 - Therefore if any man [be] in Christ, [he is] a new creature: old things are passed away; behold, all things are become new.

John 8:34 - Jesus answered them, Verily, verily, I say unto you, Whosoever committeth sin is the servant of sin.

1 Corinthians 6:9-10 - Know ye not that the unrighteous shall not inherit the kingdom of God? Be not deceived: neither fornicators, nor idolaters, nor adulterers, nor effeminate, nor abusers of themselves with mankind,

Temptations

1 Corinthians 10:13 - There hath no temptation taken you but such as is common to man: but God [is] faithful, who will not suffer you to be tempted above that ye are able; but will with the temptation also make a way to escape, that ye may be able to bear [it].

Matthew 26:41 - Watch and pray, that ye enter not into temptation: the spirit indeed [is] willing, but the flesh [is] weak.

James 1:12-16 - Blessed [is] the man that endureth temptation: for when he is tried, he shall receive the crown of life, which the Lord hath promised to them that love him. (Read More...)

Hebrews 2:18 - For in that he himself hath suffered being tempted, he is able to succour them that are tempted.

Matthew 4:1-11 - Then was Jesus led up of the Spirit into the wilderness to be tempted of the devil.

Mark 14:38 - Watch ye and pray, lest ye enter into temptation. The spirit truly [is] ready, but the flesh [is] weak.

Unity

Philippians 2:2 - Fulfil ye my joy, that ye be likeminded, having the same love, [being] of one accord, of one mind.

1 Peter 3:8 - Finally, [be ye] all of one mind, having compassion one of another, love as brethren, [be] pitiful, [be] courteous:

1 Corinthians 1:10 - Now I beseech you, brethren, by the name of our Lord Jesus Christ, that ye all speak the same thing, and [that] there be no divisions among you; but [that] ye be perfectly joined together in the same mind and in the same judgment.

2 Corinthians 13:11 - Finally, brethren, farewell. Be perfect, be of good comfort, be of one mind, live in peace; and the God of love and peace shall be with you.

Romans 15:6 - That ye may with one mind [and] one mouth glorify God, even the Father of our Lord Jesus Christ.

Romans 12:4-5 - For as we have many members in one body, and all members have not the same office:

Ephesians 4:3 - Endeavouring to keep the unity of the Spirit in the bond of peace.

Philippians 1:27 - Only let your conversation be as it becometh the gospel of Christ: that whether I come and see you, or else be absent, I may hear of your affairs, that ye stand fast in one spirit, with one mind striving together for the faith of the gospel;

Romans 14:19 - Let us therefore follow after the things which make for peace, and things wherewith one may edify another.

Acts 4:32 - And the multitude of them that believed were of one heart and of one soul: neither said any [of them] that ought of the things which he possessed was his own; but they had all things common.

Romans 12:16 - [Be] of the same mind one toward another. Mind not high things, but condescend to men of low estate. Be not wise in your own conceits.

Romans 15:5 - Now the God of patience and consolation grant you to be likeminded one toward another according to Christ Jesus:

Ephesians 4:13 - Till we all come in the unity of the faith, and of the knowledge of the Son of God, unto a perfect man, unto the measure of the stature of the fulness of Christ:

Wisdom

James 1:5 - If any of you lack wisdom, let him ask of God, that giveth to all [men] liberally, and upbraideth not; and it shall be given him.

James 3:17 - But the wisdom that is from above is first pure, then peaceable, gentle, [and] easy to be intreated, full of mercy and good fruits, without partiality, and without hypocrisy.

Ephesians 5:15-17 - See then that ye walk circumspectly, not as fools, but as wise,

---

Proverbs 3:13-18 - Happy [is] the man [that] findeth wisdom, and the man [that] getteth understanding.

Proverbs 10:23 - [It is] as sport to a fool to do mischief: but a man of understanding hath wisdom.

Proverbs 12:15 - The way of a fool [is] right in his own eyes: but he that hearkeneth unto counsel [is] wise.

Proverbs 18:15 - The heart of the prudent getteth knowledge; and the ear of the wise seeketh knowledge.

Colossians 3:16 - Let the word of Christ dwell in you richly in all wisdom; teaching and admonishing one another in psalms and hymns and spiritual songs, singing with grace in your hearts to the Lord.

Proverbs 17:27-28 - He that hath knowledge spareth his words: [and] a man of understanding is of an excellent spirit.

Proverbs 19:20 - Hear counsel, and receive instruction, that thou mayest be wise in thy latter end.

Ecclesiastes 8:1 - Who [is] as the wise [man]? and who knoweth the interpretation of a thing? a man's wisdom maketh his face to shine, and the boldness of his face shall be changed.

Books Written by Doc Yeager:

"Living in the Realm of the Miraculous #1"

"I need God Cause I'm Stupid"

"The Miracles of Smith Wigglesworth"

"How Faith Comes 28 WAYS"

"Horrors of Hell, Splendors of Heaven"

"The Coming Great Awakening"

"Sinners In The Hands of an Angry GOD", "(modernized)"

"Brain Parasite Epidemic"

"My JOURNEY To HELL" - illustrated for teenagers

"Divine Revelation Of Jesus Christ"

"My Daily Meditations"

"Holy Bible of JESUS CHRIST"

"War In The Heavenlies - (Chronicles of Micah)"

"Living in the Realm of the Miraculous #2"

"My Legal Rights To Witness"

"Why We (MUST) Gather!- 30 Biblical Reasons"

"My Incredible, Supernatural, Divine Experiences"

"Living in the Realm of the Miraculous #3"

"How GOD Leads & Guides! - 20 Ways"

ABOUT THE AUTHOR

Dr. Michael and Kathleen Yeager have served as pastors/apostles, missionaries, evangelists, broadcasters and authors for over four decades. They flow in the gifts of the Holy Spirit, teaching the Word of God with wonderful signs and miracles following in confirmation of God's Word. In 1983, they began Jesus is Lord Ministries International, Biglerville, PA 17307.

Websites Connected to Doc Yeager

www.docyeager.com

www.jilmi.org

www.wbntv.org

Made in the USA
Las Vegas, NV
05 December 2023